Authors:

Tobias Ebner & Levin Granitza

— THE —
SEO
BOOK

The way to Nr. 1

EDISON
VERLAG

Imprint

Edison Verlag
Rennweg 1
93049 Regensburg
Germany

Printed by:
Amazon Media EU S.à r.l.
5 Rue Plaetis
L-2338, Luxembourg

Congratulations!

We would like to congratulate you on the purchase of the book. You have taken the 1st right step to improve the ranking of your website. You will also receive a **free SEO analysis** in this book version. You can request the SEO analysis here:

www.seomarkt.de/premium

To open the page you need the following password: **SEO2019DE89**

CONTENT

4.0 Voice Search – optimization of website content for voice searches   101

5.0 Content Marketing and the relationship between Search Engine Optimization   113

6.0 The role of social media for better marketing in the context of Search Engine Optimization   120

Introduction - Definition of SEO

1.0

BASIC UNDERSTANDING

SEO is an abbreviation that has gained a high degree of popularity among both professional website designers and private individuals who run their own homepage in their spare time. The abbreviation stands for Search Engine Optimization. The following chapter is suitable for operators of online content who monitor it, earn money with it and advertise the provided content via the Google search engine. Founders of a young and dynamic start-up company, webmasters of various websites, SEO experts who work in an advertising agency or self-taught SEO professionals can use the complete book to repeat, look up or broaden their knowledge. Interested webmasters, who are responsible for the creation, organization and maintenance of a website, get an overview of the basics of search engine optimization. This book presents simple explained instructions. It helps webmasters with a correct application to improve their ranking many times over. SEO experts who follow the advice below can also help search engines better crawl, index and understand website content. Those who put these instructions into practice can look forward to an enviable top position on their website. Furthermore, website operators who follow the instructions will increase their chances of making it into the top 3 search result pages on Google. The SEO-Markt GmbH has helped its customers to succeed with the tips and tricks in this manual. In addition, the company's consistently positive ratings provide evidence of the start-up's excellent performance. With its expertise, the company has helped its customers to position among the top 3. Therefore, this book shares with its readers the secrets and practices used by the SEO-Markt Deutschland agency for successful search engine optimization. Thus, these instructions are professional tips that have proven themselves in practice several times. In addition, beginners who have just started to create, organize and manage their website, as well as professionals who have been creating an online presence for a long time, can use this book as a guide. Search engine optimization usually involves minor changes to certain parts of a website. These are only minimal improvements, but they have a big impact on Google search. However, this only applies if webmasters combine SEO with other optimizations in a meaningful way. In this way they improve the user experience and performance of the respective homepage in the organic search results many times over. The optimization of websites is oriented to the needs of the users. Although it may seem a bit strange at first glance, the search engine is also one of the users. In turn it helps other users to discover the website content provided. The goal of search engine optimization is a comprehensible presentation of the website content. The following optimization topics impress with their universal character, as they are equally valid for websites of all sizes and types.

At the beginning of their SEO optimization, webmasters ask themselves whether their page can be found at all in the Google index (see chapter 1.3). To check this, they perform a search with the URL of the home page of their home page. In the event of a successful search result, the website will appear in the index. However, the case of an untraceable page can also occur, even if Google crawls several billion pages (see chapter 1.3). The reasons for an untraceable site are various. This can be partly due to a lack of links to other homepages. If the publication date was not long ago, Google didn't get the chance to crawl the site. Failure to find a page can also be due to a complicated structure or content that is difficult to access. Google will also not display pages if it receives error messages when crawling. Policies can also block homepage crawling using Google.

1.2

HOW THE GOOGLE RANKS WORKS

The majority of Internet users believe to actively control their search on Google. Many people do not know that the search engine made a selection long before you entered your search. Google has various ranking systems that search several billion websites within a few seconds in order to provide users with the most relevant answers to their search queries. The system performs a practical word analysis for this purpose. Numerous language models decipher the meaning of the entered terms and browse the search index for the desired words. Clever search algorithms in combination with the mentioned language models take over these tasks. Nowadays, Google not only detects spelling mistakes, but also helps users solve complicated tasks by assigning the type of search query to a specific category. The search engine uses a system for

synonyms. The term synonym stands for a word that has several meanings. The Google system mentioned, understands what the user is looking for, even if the search term entered has several meanings. Computer scientists have invested more than half a decade in the development of this system. Their efforts have paid off, however, with search results improving by more than 30 percent. In addition, the Google search algorithm differentiates whether the query is a specific term or a general question. The search engine looks for words that provide valuable clues. These include pictures, reviews and opening hours. In addition, the algorithms can differentiate whether the user is looking for today's results or rather looking for information about an organization located in his environment.

CRAWLING AND INDEXING AS THE CORNERSTONES OF GOOGLE SEARCH (HOW DOES GOOGLE GET INFORMATION?)

The term "crawling" comes from English and in this context stands for the "rolling" of a synchronous and asynchronous machine. The so-called web crawler bundles information from several billion websites, which it chronologically arranges in Google's index according to their relevance within a few seconds. The process starts with an enumeration of different websites of the former crawlings and sitemaps, which were submitted by homepage owners. In the first step, the crawlers call the Web pages and then follow the links to the relevant pages. In addition, the task of the software is to check whether more up-to-date websites are available, whether significant changes have been made to the existing websites and whether obsolete links are represented.

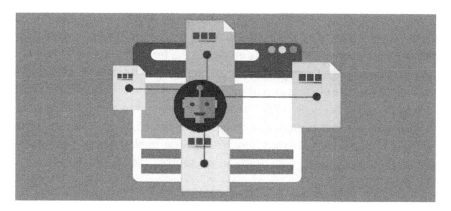

Breakdown of Search Engine marketing

In addition, the special crawling software determines which websites it searches, when and how often. It also determines how many of the numerous subpages of the respective website it calls up. The Google Search Console includes several webmaster tools. These allow website developers to determine exactly how Google should crawl their site. They give specific information to the respective sides of their homepage. Furthermore, they can ask Google to crawl their URLs again or, if they wish, prevent the crawling of their website. The search engine does not demand any monetary consideration from the users in order to "crawl" their homepages more often. It offers all website owners the same tools to ensure the best possible search results for users.

The Internet symbolizes a virtual library. Experts speak of a lending library with several billion books that is growing daily, but which is not subject to a central catalog system. For this reason, the web crawler searches for special software and websites that are accessible to the general public. The so-called crawlers go to their selected pages and visit the placed links. The process can be levelled with conventional Internet surfing. The crawlers jump from one link to another. They then send the relevant information to the Google servers. If the crawler searches successfully, the website content appears as in a browser of an Internet presence. The clever helpers examine the most relevant elements. To these belong the keywords as well as the topicality of the homepage. They then note these in the search index. The Google search index contains several billion websites and is 100 million gigabytes in size.

It works analogously to an index of a printed book. Each individual term found by the crawler is entered. During the indexing process, the search engine adds the respective web page to all the entries in the terms found on the homepage. The Knowledge Graph serves as a valuable tool to make people, places and things that are of great importance to the user easier to understand. That is why Google indexes not only website information, but also other types of information. For this reason, Google is able to search through reports from millions of books in numerous libraries, provide public transport timetable information, and provide data from various sources such as the World Bank.

BUILDING A CAMPAIGN FOR SEARCH ENGINE OPTIMIZATION

Enterprises can only survive in the free economy if they fight for comparative as well as competitive advantages. To do this, they need products or services that are tailored to customer needs, and profit-oriented organizations need a solid customer base and potential new customers. The times in which word-of-mouth propaganda was effective have long been a thing of the past. The digital landscape has meanwhile won the battle as the best advertising measure. Online campaigns are now the standard tool for developing the existing customer base. They can also improve customer service, increase and generate traffic. In addition, online campaigns act as feedback improvement. The structure of the respective representation plays a decisive role in the search engine optimization of the temporary company.

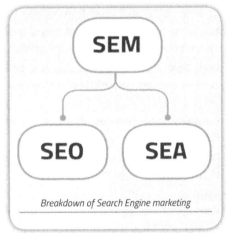

Breakdown of Search Engine marketing

Search engine marketing (SEM) has proven to be a successful tool for a successful search engine optimization campaign over the past few years. SEM stands for the implementation of all marketing measures that companies carry out in the search engines in order to increase their level of awareness as well as their services and products in the perception of customers. The SEM is now of great importance for all companies, as they definitely have to move in the digital world in order to survive in the market. Furthermore, profit-oriented organizations increase their turnover if they place a high value on a proper online presence. SEM makes a major contribution to the task of bringing products and services to the end consumer. In addition, entrepreneurs increase the number of visitors to their websites many times over. Online and offline advertisements act as effective tools. SEM acts as one of three pillars in online marketing. Search engine marketing is a combination of search engine optimization (SEO) and search engine advertising (SEA). Marketing experts also refer to the latter area as affiliate marketing. This defines the partnership between a seller and the operator of a website. SEM is the generic term for SEO and SEA. The latter aims to optimize the visibility of page content. Targeted advertising links that are close to matching search terms act as aids. In addition, both approaches have other advantages, such as successful measurement of the results. In the following, the structure of an SEO campaign is presented.

Building a Successful SEO Campaign

SEO campaigns aim to increase website ranking, traffic and conversion rates. It should be noted that the summarized advice serves as guidance for creating a successful SEO campaign. Since August 2018 Google has released a new Core Update. Accordingly, since this update the three ranking factors expertise, authority and trust have been among the decisive factors for a successful website. An SEO campaign requires website operators to increase these three factors within the website.

A successful campaign begins with good preparation. Before website operators define their content and time goals, they first define their target group through personas. However, keywords take second place. They make up a large part of the SEO strategy. Web designers use the keywords to determine which topics their users want to find them on. The persons in charge create search phrases, which would enter their personas in the search engines, in order to find the respective products, services as well as web page contents. The use of a keyword planner is recommended for the appropriate key-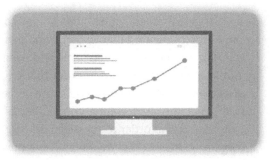

words. The second chapter of this book contains detailed instructions for the successful use of suitable keywords. Web designers, however, should focus on questions that users might ask rather than individual keywords when using keywords.

However, SEO campaigns are not only characterized by carefully selected keywords, but also by well structured content. Blogs have become one of the most important content tools for companies. However, their success depends primarily on the content. Blogs establish organizations as specialists do in their field. With the help of the selected keywords, however, webmasters can create their blog content and write helpful articles with regard to their personas' questions. For example, craft businesses can write a blog article about the installation of a window. It is worth answering the question: "How do I install a window?". Interesting and informative articles definitely stand up better to the competition. After the publication of the respective blog article, a promotion via social media channels should begin. After all, good content also deserves attention-grabbing advertising. Well-structured SEO campaigns, however, contain a flawless back link building strategy. They are an important factor in Google search. Websites profit from a higher ranking by means of a good link building. However, webmasters should always keep in mind the information "Quality is more important than quantity". In this book, interested webmasters receive a well-founded guide on how they can better rank their page in the organic search. Those who successfully put this advice into practice will benefit from this free advertising campaign. A high ranking position is comparable to good advertising. However, webmasters also have the opportunity to improve their search results by paying for them. Therefore, this book contains exclusive bonus material that explains step-by-step to web designers how to use paid search results.

However, webmasters need to get familiar with the way Google and its clever helpers work in order to optimize their website so that it appears as high up as possible. An SEO campaign is the synonym for a campaign on the Internet. After all, webmasters pursue the goal of asserting themselves against their competitors. For this reason an intensive discussion with Google's helpers is worthwhile. These are so-called bots that fulfill an important function in Google ranking. That is why they deserve an intense argument. They are described in detail in the following chapter along with their functions.

1.5

GOOGLE AND ITS CLEVER HELPERS - GOOGLE BOTS

Google Bots are indispensable tools when it comes to reading websites. Your name goes back to Google and the technical name is Bot. The second term is an abbreviation for Robot. It is already mentioned that web crawlers represent the specific type of bots. They also call themselves Searchbots. Thanks to their unique programming, they can browse the Internet and analyze websites. Google relies on its bot to help its searches succeed. The robot proves its existence with a specific user agent identifier Google Bot 2.1. The Google Bot travels from link to link to locate web pages. The content then ends up in the Google index depending on its relevance. That is why checking the Google Bots is an important step for placing a website in search results on Google. However, the Google Bot for web search is not the only one of its kind.

There are also Google Bot-News, Google Bot-Video and Google Bot-Mobile, which owes its existence to today's smartphone websites. If one of the bots mentioned has only recently crawled a Web page, it stores the content for the other crawlers in a cache. Google Bots play a decisive role in search engine optimization, which will be explained in detail in the following chapters. Google's market share is more than 90 percent. For indexing, however, the crawling process through the Google Bots plays the main role. It depends on several factors how often will the bot visit a website. On the left determine its frequency of movement. For this reason, both the page ranks and the number and quality of the existing backlinks are decisive. However, this only applies until the Google Bot crawls the page again. Loading times and website structures as well as update frequencies of the page contents play an important role during the crawling process. Pages equipped with numerous and advantageous backlinks can be read by the Google Bot every ten seconds. Smaller pages, on the other hand, can wait up to a month or even longer to be indexed by Google.

With regard to a search engine optimized marketing, website operators definitely cannot avoid the inclusion of their site in the Google Index. This procedure is essential for finding a page in the search results. The Google Crawler uses different elements to index a page. Therefore a good ON-Page SEO is indispensable for a firm place in the Google index. ON-Page SEO includes the creation and optimization of website content.

The linking to other meaningful websites and URLs is another important criterion. Compliance with this condition is of great importance for the Google Bot. In this way the own homepage increases its degree of popularity.

 Tip:

Do not forget your free SEO-Analysis for further information.
Get it now **www.seomarkt.de/premium**
Password: **SEO2019DE89**

The way to the top position in the search index

2.0

T his chapter begins with the keyword search, as it occupies an funda- mental place in the design of a page that is in the top position in the search index. The quality guidelines are then presented. Web admin- istrators must adhere to these in order to benefit from a sustainable ranking. The next step is a detailed presentation of the necessary changes to a website, which increase the ranking many times over. These are on-page SEO measures. However, the topic called Pagespeed has its own subchapter because it is invaluable, even if it is a building block of ON-Page search engine optimization. According to these informative instructions, the structured data are happy about an extensive dedication, as they also improve the ranking of a website. Beyond that the OFF-Page SEO is explained in detail, because this is not to be excluded from a successful search machine optimization no more.

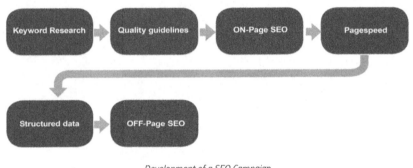

Development of a SEO Campaign

2.1

KEYWORD RESEARCH

Keyword research is an elementary function in search engine optimization. Without this activity the success of a website is definitely doomed to failure. Keywords are keywords with which both webmasters and users associate an Internet presence. These must therefore be chosen with care. Furthermore, web designers slip into the role of their website visitors during keyword re- search. They locate phrases and keywords that users enter in search engines.

Then they place them in a clever way in their online presence in order to appear as high as possible in the organic (unpaid) search results. The challenge, however, is to find the right keywords that are popular with users but stand out from the competition. That is why webmasters receive detailed instructions in this chapter on how to find the right keywords and how to improve their website accordingly.

2.1.1 Finding the right keywords for successful search engine optimization

The keyword research of search engine optimization stands for the search for a suitable keyword to a website. Users use the selected keyword to locate the particular page on the Internet. Accordingly, the choice of the keyword plays the leading role. However, this should not only match the website content, but should also be searched for by the selected target group. However, the term keyword does not only stand for a single keyword, but also defines a text unit that can either be found in the text or briefly represents the content of the text as a suitable keyword. Accordingly, keywords are created from several terms and numbers. They are representatives for terms, about which a text is found at best with Google as well as further search engines. The biggest challenge for webmasters lies in their ability to put themselves in their target group. In practice, it often happens that websites are optimized for unsuitable keywords because the target group uses completely different names than the website operator. The aim of keyword research is to find the words that the majority of the target group members are looking for.

2.1.2 Types of keywords

There are different types of keywords. With regard to the intention of the users, keywords can be divided into three different groups. These consist of commercial, informative and navigating keywords.
Commercial keywords enter the users who have a purchase intention. A classic example of this would be "Buying a Travel Guide to the USA". Those who sell the product they are looking for should choose their keywords carefully and always be careful to signal the intention to buy.
When choosing the keywords "Travel Tips USA", however, users who enter these terms have the intention of receiving free travel tips. Thus, the main intention of this user is definitely not to visit a paid travel guide. However, providers who offer an article with free travel tips for the USA and want to advertise their travel guide at the end of the text can use this keyword.

Users searching for information on a specific topic use informative keywords. The question: "How big is the Eiffel Tower?" is a classic example of the use of informative keywords. Such questions are also ideal for Voice SEO. This book contains an additional chapter on this subject. Webmasters who use these keywords will definitely not find any users who have a purchase intention.

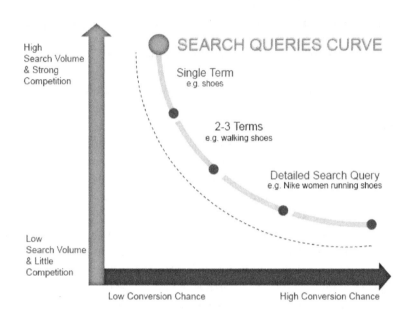

Graphical display of search volume and keyword length

Navigation-oriented keywords are terms entered by users who know a product or service. In this case, users only search for a suitable page or subpage. "Apple Store Munich" is a typical example of a navigation-oriented keyword combination.

Webmasters looking for the right keywords should always keep the three types of keywords in mind.

Finally, the keywords can be differentiated according to the distinguishing feature of length. With regard to length, keyword forms such as short, head tail, mid tail and tail are available.

Short or head tail keywords consist of only one term. Even though this keyword species is a non-specific genus, it covers a huge spectrum.

Mid tail key words mainly contain two to three terms and represent the middle of the extremely unspecific short tail and specific long tail keywords.

Long tail keywords usually contain more than four terms. This keyword is a specific type of keyword that becomes more and more exact thanks to the addition of additional terms.

An example of a short or head tail keyword would be the term "bread". The mid tail keyword extension could be "bake bread". The final long tail keyword might be "bake bread at home".

2.1.3   The distinction between good and bad keywords

Before the instructions for a successful keyword search are dealt with, the distinction between good and bad keywords is made.

An online retailer who sells outerwear such as T-shirts, jackets or pullovers would probably at first glance choose the keyword "outerwear", which is theoretically perfectly correct, but in practice less well received by the searcher. The question is whether the target group is actually looking for "outerwear". The answer is rather no. The keyword "outerwear" is a Head Tail Keyword, which is not commercial. Even if it could achieve a high search volume, the number of connections would be extremely low because this keyword is too inaccurate. The keywords "T-shirt" or "jacket" do not represent a suitable alternative either, because they do not indicate which target the searchers are aiming for, because they are not a commercial keyword. If the individuals want to make a purchase, they will rather enter the keywords "buy jacket" (commercial keyword). Online merchants who only rank their shop for the term "jacket" by no means address their desired target group directly. The keyword research thus aims at a precise formulation and exact alignment of the keywords.

In general, the principle applies: "The more general a keyword is, the greater the number of suitable pages Google will find". At the same time, this leads to enormous competition. As a result, the online retailer's chance of getting to the first page, who only ranked his shop after the keyword "jacket", drops considerably. Therefore a keyword, which describes the respective offer of the side as exactly as possible, should be the main goal. However, it should be a commercial keyword. In this way, entrepreneurs reach their target group with significantly less effort.

2.1.4 Recommendation of keyword species

In order to find suitable keywords, the knowledge of the correct keyword type is absolutely necessary. At times, long tail keywords dominated search engine optimization. This is partly due to the small number of competitors. That is why website operators can quickly move up to the top rank of search queries. However, the problem with long tail keywords lies in their search volume. A search volume of 100 is not enough to be successful with a website. For this reason, an optimization of similar long tail keywords and related texts takes place using different keywords. Therefore it is not recommended that a page presents five individual web pages with the same topic but optimized with different long tail keywords. This increases the search volume. However, this strategy has had its day. Google is now extremely clever and recognizes these tricks. This strategy came to an end at the latest with the so-called Panda Update. For this reason, website operators rank only as a single long tail keyword, which however reduces the search volume. The following overview summarizes the disadvantages of long tail keywords.

✓ Latest updates prevent Google ranking of different pages on the same topic.
✓ The search volume is extremely small.
✓ Contributions of inferior quality have a negative impact on the authority of the website.

Due to the mentioned disadvantages it is worthwhile to switch to Mid Tail Keywords. Even if these are highly competitive, with a good choice and consistent content promotion, they can quickly catapult a website into the top ranks. However, the competition is the greatest with short tail keywords. But webmasters reach the largest number of users with this keyword type. However, practice has proven that short tail keywords are not the right choice. Therefore Mid Tail Keywords are best suited. Their competition is limited. This is partly because they are not as general as short tail keywords. In addition, they increase the probability of a financial statement.

A carefully conducted keyword research saves the webmasters not only time, but also money. A suitable keyword is the prerequisite for earning money. Unsuitable keywords that do not match the website content do not provide added value for the searcher. In addition, careful webmasters with a good keyword research can find keywords that competitors do not use. In this way, webmasters benefit from the comparative competitive advantages. In the following chapter the keyword research is presented with the help of free tools.

2.1.5 Suitable methods and structured procedures for keyword research

The following keyword search can be done with Google. Webmasters do not need any tools with costs for this manual. Accordingly, the displayed keyword research is free of charge.

1. Keyword brainstorming
2. Write down keywords that match the website in question
3. The keyword is surrounded by a cloud with matching additional terms
4. If the example keyword is "baking bread", other terms such as gluten-free, whole meal flour, sunflower bread or baguette can surround the main keyword.

In order to be able to better understand and apply these measures, the techniques described are carried out using the keyword "baking bread" as an example.

Keyword Input into a suitable keyword tool

The following instructions are for a successful keyword search, which is carried out with Google. The Google Keyword Planner can help. Webmasters can also use other keyword tools, which they can use for free. After the tool has been selected, the keyword is entered into the selected tool. Those who want to do the keyword research with AdWords only need a Google account. The webmasters then simply enter their main term in the Keyword Planner Tool under "Search for new keywords using a phrase, a web page and a category". When you click on Ideas Retrieve, different ones are displayed.

Sorting the list in keyword search according to the respective search volume

As a result, users receive a whole list of keyword suggestions that correspond to the main term. With a click on the field called "Average search queries per month" webmasters can arrange them from large to small. The keywords that stand out due to the highest search volume appear in the upper rank. At the end or on the last result pages of this list, keywords with a small search volume are mentioned. Usually these are long tail keywords. The middle ranks are important for webmasters, as the majority of mid tail keywords are placed here. Based on this ad, website operators select a keyword that best matches the content of their online presence. It is advisable to take a look at the column called "Competition" and also to inspect the climbing pages for the respective mid tail keyword. However, since the Google Keyword Planner is an AdWords tool, the competition does not refer to the display of search results, but to general ads. For this reason webmasters may not neglect the climbing web pages to the respective keyword.

Competitive intelligence

At this step, webmasters analyze their competitors to a keyword. There are different indicators for this. The competition can serve both as an indication of how powerful the competition is and the "interrupted bid". The higher the bid, the higher the competition. However, website designers do not rely solely on this information. This is because a certain keyword is extremely expensive to display and enjoys great popularity, but is not very successful in organic search results. In order to find out how big the competition for the selected keyword is, it is worth applying the following techniques.

1. Enter the URL, the domain metrics, and a check of the backlinks.
2. Control of ON-Page Optimization
3. Check the respective search results on question-answer pages or in forums
4. Inspect content quality more closely

In order to better understand and apply these measures, the techniques described are carried out using the example keyword "baking bread".

1. **Input of the URL, the domain metrics as well as a check of the backlinks**

   In this step, webmasters use a tool that presents them with important metrics. The free tool called "SEO Toolbar" of the developer named MOZ can be helpful. It requires an installation. After the successful setup of the toolbar, the keyword input takes place at Google. Among the current results, the toolbar with all the metrics for the matching page and domain now appears without further ado. Webmasters are particularly interested in the values URL Rating, Backlinks / Linking Domains to the Website, Domain Rating and Backlinks / Linking Domains to the Complete Page.

The first step is an analysis of the URL rating. This represents the strength of a single page. In this case, the majority of the values are below 20. Ultimately, this means that competition is more in the lower range.

Webmasters should not miss the information on how this website is linked. For this reason, naming the source of the back link is indispensable. To fulfill this task, you need a so-called Back Link Checker. Those who do not have a tool that can display backlinks to a domain can choose a free tool.

When analyzing the back link of a page that is ranked first, experts advise you to consider the following aspects. Based on the domain rating, webmasters read that strong domains link to this page. As a rule, these are topic-relevant websites. For example, the link type overview shows that of the 41 backlinks, only one is marked "NoFollow". Therefore almost all backlinks are of high quality. Google attaches great importance to the content presented. The site, which has taken first place, offers users an informative contribution in which they can also find general information on the subject of "baking bread". Finally, the metrics for the respective domains are analyzed. If almost all of them have a domain rating of over 50 and only thousands or even several million backlinks, webmasters should realize that they can only compete with other websites with difficulty on this keyword.

2.   Control of OnPage Optimization

Since ON-Page Optimization is an important aspect of search engine optimization, many pages that have not been optimized point to low competition. With the ON-Page Optimization Control, webmasters take a closer look at the search results. You check whether the selected keyword is present in the title tags. Almost all entries use the keyword "buy food supplements". In order to get to the bottom of this fact, webmasters should nevertheless take a closer look at the individual pages. Important hints for optimization are provided, for example:

✓ Keyword placement in H1 + H2 headings
✓ Keyword placement in the respective URL

Web designers have the option to view the website and manually perform the ON-Page Optimization check or use OneProSEO's free SEO Check Tool. This performs the control of the ON-Page optimization.

If the keyword should appear in the URL as well as in the numerous H1 headings, except in the H2 headings, this does not mean that the page was optimized badly. Webmasters should take this step to control the first top ten websites. If they find one or two pages that have not been optimized, they can consider this indication as an indicator of a keyword with little competition.

3. **Check the respective search results on question-answer pages or in forums.**

For some keywords, questions from question-answer pages or forums such as "gutefrage.net" can also appear in the Top 10. This notice proves how inadequately the competitors' site has been optimized in relation to this keyword.

4. **Inspect content quality more closely.**

The step of controlling content quality is the most important aspect of keyword research. Webmasters take a close look at the contents of the individual pages. If they find predominantly modest information or boring and much too short articles on the subject of "buying dietary supplements", this provides a clear indication of weak competition. However, if the articles on this topic are exclusively long and informative, then it is definitely a strong keyword. For this reason, it is worth searching for an alternative keyword. The already mentioned profile can serve as an important aid.

The keyword planner from Google

People searching for a keyword in Google's Keyword Planner now find the exact number of keywords and the corresponding search volume in the relevant column. Google's Keyword Planner allows its users to continue to check the exact search volume. But for that they have to accept some obstacles.

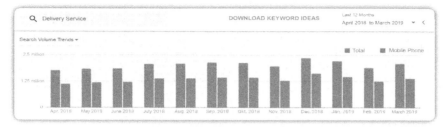

Searchvolume trends over time

✓ In the first step webmasters select the function "Determine new keywords". They then perform an ordinary search for a keyword.

Start screen of the Google Keyword Planner

✓ After that, webmasters should make sure that they have selected the target region Germany. The default setting always refers to the USA. Therefore it is important to observe this setting. After clicking on the target region and the corresponding language, users can enjoy a German version.

The keyword planner now displays a list with the search volume and the search term. It provides meaningful ideas for keywords that webmasters can use. In addition, the users receive information regarding keywords of the advertisements of their competitors. However, they should not adopt them one-to-one under any circumstances. A detailed explanation in this regard follows on the following pages.

Keywords (by relevance) ↓	Average search queries per month	Competition
Search Terms		
delivery service	60.500	Medium
Keyword Ideas		
pizza order	49.500	Medium
pizza delivery service	18.100	Low
pizza service	9.900	Low
pizza delivery	8.100	Low
delivery service	14.800	Low
pizza service	9.900	Low
pizza taxi	5.400	Low
order pizza online	1.900	Medium
delievery service pizza	720	Low
bring service	1.900	Low
online delivery service	480	Medium
pizza bring service	1.900	Low

Keyword ideas including searchvolume

Tip:

For some webmasters the information about the distribution of keywords in relation to the respective federal states might be interesting. All you have to do is select "Breakdown by location"in the upper left corner. You can also use this tab to display how the keywords are distributed across end devices (mobile phones, tablet PCs and desktops).

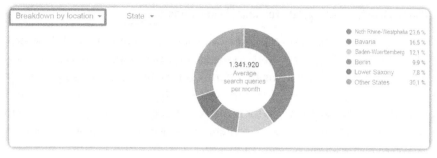

Search volume: Breakdown by location

FURTHER STRATEGIES FOR KEYWORD RESEARCH

Webmasters who, despite the methods described above, have difficulty finding the perfect keyword can acquire the following alternative strategies.

Use forums as idea suppliers for keywords

Forums represent a suitable opportunity for keyword research. On these pages webmasters directly meet the questions and problems of their target group. You can get first class information about the difficulties of the customers. In the example of buying dietary supplements, consumers often feel insecure about the quality of the products. To find suitable forums, webmasters should enter their "keyword" + "forum" in the Google search. Those who still have not been able to commit to a single keyword should use this approach with different keywords. After Google input, the forums are browsed and a more detailed analysis of the questions and answers of the target group for the respective keyword is carried out. Interesting terms are noted. Then there is a skip to the second and third step from the technique of successful keyword research with the respective designations.

Use Wikipedia as a template for suitable keywords

Not only forums, but also Wikipedia can support webmasters with keyword research. In this huge online encyclopedia, numerous people make the daily effort to classify contributions to different terms into suitable categories. All webmasters need to do is call up the "wikpedia.de" website and enter the keyword they would like to search for in the search bar at the top right. For search engine optimization, the table of contents is particularly interesting because it can provide crucial ideas.

Related searches from Google

Webmasters can, for example, enter the term "search engine optimization" in Google and scroll to the bottom of the page. There you will see the "relatives search queries". Thanks to this function, motivated website designers can quickly and easily find mid tail keywords that are directly linked to a large short tail keyword and could therefore be great as their main keyword.

Amazon as inspiration for keywords

Amazon also acts as a good keyword search help. Webmasters enter their keyword in the Amazon search under the heading "Books". They then receive a long list of specialist literature. Sometimes just a single title is

Similar search queries for headphones

headphones test winner	headphones bad
headphones in ear	headphones teufel
headphones bluetooth	headphones cables
headphones media market	headphones jbl

enough to supply ideas. However, if this is not the case, a "look into the book" can also help. The table of contents provides valuable hints for new keywords. Of course, website owners can also enter the selected keywords into the Google Keyword Planner to discover a suitable mid tail keyword for their website.

Google Suggest - the free keyword research tool

The Google Suggest function is a term for everyone, thanks to their own search queries. Searchers receive automated suggestions when they enter a keyword into Google. Accordingly, a single keyword is transformed into a mid-tail keyword. The question that arises here is how this function can be turned into a free keyword research tool. The advantage of this feature is that mid tail keywords, which are very popular, are displayed first. However, in order not to enter all keywords at Google, webmasters use the Suggest function. That is where they enter their cue. They then select the appropriate country and language. Then click on Suggest and get the best Mid Tail Keywords.

The optimization of keywords

Optimizing keywords should be a habit for webmasters that they regularly follow. In this way, they ensure that the good keywords are not overlooked. For the optimization of a page to a suitable keyword, it is worthwhile to work through the chapter of ON-Page Optimization repeatedly.

Conclusion

This chapter explains in detail which properties a perfect keyword has. It is a good mixture of search volume and competition and reflects exactly the content the target group needs. Furthermore, the three different keyword types are no longer unknown terrain. The challenge is to always choose the right keyword for the respective page. This procedure helps to find the appropriate keyword. If the searchers do not find the information they are looking for on a website, they logically jump to the next website. But the keywords are not the only component that is important for a search engine optimized text. The structure of the page and the texts also plays an important role.

BEFORE CONTINUING: OBSERVE QUALITY GUIDELINES

Web masters can draw with Google from the free and simple admission of their homepage a high use. Furthermore, they do not even need to submit their site to the well-known search engine. This is due to Google's fully automated search function, which uses web crawlers to constantly search the Internet for web pages to add to the index. The majority of the pages in Google did not enjoy active submission of their webmasters. The search engine automatically detected them and added them during crawling. There are interesting guidelines on the net that speak in favour of creating a Google-friendly website. However, meeting the conditions does not provide any guarantee for the appearance of the respective website on Google. Since they do, however, provide a helpful orientation function, a description of the respective webmaster guidelines is given below.

There are guidelines that make it easy to find the site. Conversely, however, there are also illegal procedures that cause a certain page to be permanently removed from the Google index. This is especially true for spam measures. Such pages do not benefit from a Google ad. Furthermore, they are also blocked by Google's partner websites.

Observe quality guidelines – ensure success in ON-Page SEO

Quality guidelines fulfil several purposes at the same time. They serve to cover any form of manipulation. Google also recognizes other methods that prove misleading in practice. The search engine rewards home page designers with a better ranking when they create websites that are user friendly. Spam websites are rarely found in Google search. Those who have escaped Google's watchful eye will nevertheless sooner or later be out of the ranking. For this reason, webmasters should adhere to the following basic rules when creating their websites. You create a page for users and not for Google. A deliberate deception during the optimization process strikes back like a boomerang and in the worst case leads to a removal from the Google ranking. Experienced homepage designers know how unnecessary tricks are which improve the search engine ranking.

A good point of reference for creating a successful website is to ask yourself whether a competitor or a Google employee would like the methods used if they received a detailed explanation from the webmaster responsible. Other useful questions that can help you create websites are Does my site offer serious benefits to readers? Would I act like this if it weren't for Google or other search engines? The consideration of whether the homepage is unique, valuable and attractive at the same time provides a helpful indication of a good website design. The site is special if it stands out from the competition that offers a similar product or service.

The following advice is intended as helpful information that webmasters should avoid in order to increase the success of their site. Content that has been created by an automation process is one of the measures homepage designers should keep away from. Google can mercilessly remove search rankings that offer no advantages to users. These include, among other things, a text that does not offer the reader valuable added value, but merely contains search terms that are arranged in series. Texts that have been translated into another language by an automatic translator such as Google or another tool are also absolute knock-out texts. Translated articles must be corrected and edited before publication. They offer linguistically, grammatically and content-wise impeccable content. Translators whose passion is the daily handling of several languages can see at a glance whether only one tool or one person has translated a contribution. Homepages that publish reports created by automatic obfuscation do not reach the user either. Formulations that owe their existence to Atom or RSS feeds appear as little in search results as automated and incorrect translations. Those who disregard the copyright of other articles and simply merge or combine web content from different websites without adding their own thoughts, also search in vain for their copied versions.

Among the other methods that webmasters should avoid is participation in so-called link exchange programs. These are links that manipulate the ranking of a homepage in the search engines. Google defines link exchange programs as a policy violation. The unauthorized measures consist of links that either lead to or emanate from a website. The following list illustrates the link exchange programs that have a negative effect on Google search. The monetary exchange for special links or posts as well as the bartering of goods or services for certain links is one of the measures that successful webmasters avoid.

Sending toll-free products or services when users write a positive review and then add a link is also one of the ways to keep webmasters successful. An intensive link exchange business as well as a mutual linking of partner websites do not have a positive effect on the Google ranking either. An intensive article marketing in an extensive style as well as the posting of campaigns as visitors with targeted anchor text links, which are also characterized by a keyword spam, are also out of place. Fraudsters who cheat their way into the top ranks resort to automated programs or services to create links to their homepage. But this measure is not recommended for Google or other search engines.

Unnatural links are also among the offences that Google does not approve of at all. Among other things, they represent text advertisements that display PageRanks. Native advertising, which finances articles with further links that a PageRank passes on, is also one of the undesirable measures. Texts that have an optimized anchor text with further links are also misplaced. The following example illustrates this fact, where the underlined terms symbolize the unnatural links.

The supply of underlined baby clothes is enormous. If you are expecting a baby, you are looking for a high quality baby store. You will also need a cot and a pram.

Experienced webmasters also avoid links to directories and bookmarks of inferior quality. Hidden links or links that contain too many keywords have no place on a well-structured homepage. In practice, the proverb "Honest lasts the longest" dominates. The same principle can be applied by webmasters who want to be successful with their website. The best way for a homepage designer to do this is to get another webmaster to link to their own page with interesting content that the community can use. Educational web content pays off in many ways. Links usually require editorial assessments, which are subject to voluntary submission. In business, the principle applies that the more useful a product or service is, the more likely it is to be demanded by the masses. The same principle also applies in the Internet world. The more valuable the website content is, the more likely it is that another website operator will link its readers to the page it considers interesting.

Other concrete recommendations that companies, freelancers and individuals should avoid when creating their homepage include creating pages that have a small amount of content. Cloaking is also one of the procedures that is undesirable with a website that is supposed to score points with good search engine optimization. The term cloaking stands for various contents and URLs of a website. This is a violation of the guidelines because users do not get the same results. Those who practice cloaking provide the search engine with HTML text, while those who do display a web page with images or even Flash elements to their readers. The term has its origin in English and comes from the verb cloak, the translation of which is "veiling". Cloaking therefore also stands for webmasters who only insert keywords in their texts if the user agent is a search engine and not a real visitor. Hackers also use cloaking in their attacks to make it difficult for website owners to discover their intent.

These are described in more detail below. Furthermore, Google offers webmasters useful tools to submit their website content to the well-known search engine and to check their current status in Google search. The Search Console can send reports on questionable problems that are present on the website on request. But before webmasters use this service, they register with Google's Search Console. The following catalogue of questions also serves as a small help for the creation of a website, which then appears on Google.

- ✓ **Can I find my website using Google Search?**
- ✓ **Is my content of high quality and can users really benefit from it?**
- ✓ **Can the searchers read my company location from Google?**
- ✓ **Can my content be accessed quickly and easily on users' devices?**
- ✓ **Have I considered the visibility settings of my website?**

All website designers benefit from the free and easy inclusion of their homepage in Google. They do not even have to explicitly submit their site to the well-known search engine. This is due to the fully automatic feature of Google. The Web crawlers described above are responsible for this. Google thus automatically adds the pages to the search results when it crawls through the Internet. However, in order to appear high on Google, a good search engine optimization is required.

Therefore, the following chapter presents the elementary functions of search engine optimization.

DEVELOPE A COMPETITIVE SEO STRATEGY

The following proverb perfectly symbolizes the development of a competitive SEO strategy. Sunzi has already brought it to the point in the year 500 before Christ, when he held on to what is important in a fight. Even though he has worked as a military consultant, his knowledge can still be applied today to a successful SEO strategy.

"If you know yourself and know your enemy, in a hundred battles you will never fear the result. When you know yourself but not your enemy, your chances of winning or losing are equal. If you know neither yourself, nor your enemy, you are certain that in every battle, you will be in danger."

- Chinese Military Strategist Sunzi in 500 BC

A well thought-out SEO strategy takes the corporate environment and the competition equally into account. It takes into account the rapid technological development of search engines. In addition, a good strategy takes a close look at the strengths and weaknesses of the company's own website as well as its position in comparison to the competition. Accordingly, the strategy reflects central attitudes and desired goals.

In addition, successful SEO strategists are initially thinking about their industry. They use the following questions as an aid:

Industry analysis:
- ✓ How is the industry changing on the Internet?
- ✓ How is the behavior of Internet users within the industry changing?
- ✓ What are the industry characteristics?
- ✓ How high is demand for this industry on social media?
- ✓ Which companies are best found and why?

Subsequently, it may be helpful to perform a SWOT analysis. This helps with position determination and strategy planning. The term SWOT comes from English and stands for an analysis of strengths, weaknesses, opportunities and threats. In practice, SWOT analysis has proved to be a useful tool for planning a successful strategy. This is why it is also used in search engine optimization.

This is what an exemplary SWOT analysis looks like.

SWOT analysis:

Strengths
- ✓ domain already exists for more than one year
- ✓   the site receives regular traffic
- ✓ furthermore the page is already easy to find in connection with some keywords

Weaknesses
- ✓ Competitors are displayed above the respective website for relevant keywords.
- ✓ Pagespeed is not good
- ✓ Spamscore is high
- ✓ Bounce rate is high
- ✓ Conversation rate has low chances

Chances
- ✓ Use new sales channels
- ✓ Attract more customers through organic search
- ✓ Increase brand awareness
- ✓ Rank 1 in Google for relevant keywords risks

Risks
- ✓ Entry of new competitors into the market
- ✓ Newer SEO techniques from competitors
- ✓ Competitors want to gain market share via social media.
- ✓ Website has bad backlinks and is endangered by an upcoming Google update.

The strategy should build on existing strengths and address the weaknesses analyzed. However, if these cannot be repaired, it is necessary to overcome them. In addition, the SWOT analysis uses the opportunities identified and at the same time as the risks analyzed. In this example, we build on the regular traffic that the customer generates one after the other on his website. More over, a carefully selected content marketing strategy is used. The Domain Authority is increased with very high-quality backlinks. Since the conversation rate is low, a heatmap (tool for visualizing user interactions on the website) is installed. In this way webmasters focus on the reason of the fact. Based on this an A/B test takes place. With this approach, the conversation rate can be drastically increased in any case. Since the spam score of the respective domain is high, a back link removal is carried out while the creation of high-quality links takes place at the same time. Furthermore, the Pagespeed is also increased by technical adjustments. The most important thing is to find out why the other companies are in the first place. What strategy do they follow? In the following chapters, interested webmasters learn all the skills they need to implement such a strategy.

2.5

ON-PAGE SEO MEASURES

ON-Page SEO contains important measures which improve the success as well as the appearance of a website in the organic search results many times over. A successful search engine optimization, however, contains several steps that lead to a measurable success when executed correctly. Therefore, website operators should familiarize themselves with operators of all ON-Page SEO measures. These include compliance with important quality guidelines, a clear presentation of page content or the use of meaningful titles. Thus the following chapter is dedicated to all necessary ON-Page SEO measures, which enable web designers a successful ranking.

Before administrators get started, they should create an account on search. google.com and then verify their website. This tool will prove to be a useful tool throughout this chapter.

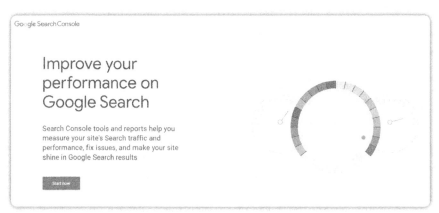

Help Google display the content you're looking for

Website administrators first check to see if they can find their own page on Google. Incidentally, this is the first step towards successful indexing. For this process, experts recommend submitting a sitemap. This acts as a file located on the website to inform search engines of new or changed pages on the existing website. There are many free online tools to create a sitemap. But what is a sitemap?

A sitemap is a file in which the individual pages of a website are listed. In this way, both Google and any other search engine obtain information about the structure of the website. In addition, the Google Bot reads this content and can crawl the page more intelligently based on the information provided. Sitemaps therefore play an important role in the indexing of a homepage. For pages that have a small number of subpages, the Google Bots have no problem crawling them, whereas for detailed web pages there is a risk that the crawlers will overlook important content or subpages. This is often the case with extensive sites such as online shops or publishing houses, as these have numerous sub-pages. Crawlers overlook important content even if the pages are not well linked to each other. New websites that have a small number of external incoming links also have this problem.

There are two types of sitemaps. They consist of an HTML sitemap and an XML sitemap. The names of the sitemaps go back to their saved file format. HTML sitemaps serve as orientation for those who visit the site. This variant works in the same way as a table of contents. The XML sitemap, on the other hand, contains information about the individual URLs and the data from the most recent updates. In addition to these two types, there are also picture, video, news and mobile sitemaps. In the meantime, the majority of CMS systems have uncomplicated sitemap functions, which is why the creation of such a page has proven to be easy in practice. In order to inform search engines about the existence of a sitemap, the robots.txt file should contain a hint about its existence.

Graphical representation of a sitemap

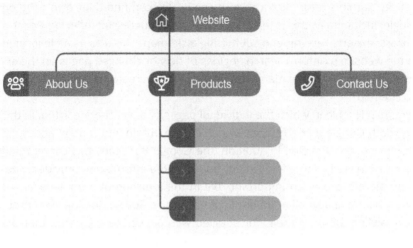

Structure of a sitemap

Users can submit the sitemap via their Google Search Console account. First upload the sitemap to your server and then open the "Sitemaps" tab in the Google Search Console. Then specify the path to the file.

The page "Sitemaps" in the Google Search Console

Robots.txt - Clarify which pages it should not crawl

There is a file called robots.txt. It informs search engines where to access and crawl certain parts of a web page. Webmasters give this file a place in the root directory of their homepage. However, it is still possible to crawl pages that are located in this This is the case. Webmasters should therefore rely on a reliable approach. The reason why some pages should not appear in Google lies in their low benefit for the respective readers. This applies in particular to subpages. These should be in the robots.txt file. However, there are other possibilities that can effectively counteract unwanted crawling. Webmasters should definitely use these, as they are logically eager for a positive feedback of their website. Web designers who neglect this minor detail will face negative reactions from their website if they do not make it clear to Google which pages it should not crawl. Otherwise, the Google Crawler is automatically redirected to another page. This means that the crawler is redirected to a page that web page designers usually do not want indexed in Google.

Users react bitterly when they find a page in the search results that is not intended for them like a semi-finished landing page. Good webmasters pro-hibit Google from crawling these pages in favor of your users. Allowing URLs created by website designers based on proxy services to be crawled is also one of the unwanted pages and subpages of a well-structured website. Web-masters must therefore use reliable methods to disclose or use confidential information. This shows how unsuitable and ineffective the robots.txt file is for blocking confidential material. This is because the file crawlers that respond to a particular behavior merely indicates that the pages were not created for them. The server can still send the pages to a browser. Search engines also have the option of using URLs blocked by the webmaster if links exist on the Internet. Reference logs that contain these links provide the best proof of this. Search engines then simply show the URL without title and snippet. Non-com-pliant or not at all allowed search engines do not consider the instructions of the robots.txt file at all. In addition, they do not recognize the standardized exclusion of the robot file. Inquisitive users are able to call up directories and subdirectories of robots.txt files themselves. For this reason, experts recom-mend the use of the tag with the name "noindex", if the respective subpage should not appear in Google search under any circumstances. However, if it is a site that requires a high level of security, webmasters should use high quality authorization methods such as using a password or completely removing the site or setting it to Private.

To create a robots.txt, webmasters use numerous free tools. Then they test the file with the robots.txt tester from Google and submit it directly.

robots.txt-Tester

Edit your robots.txt file and check if there are any errors. Future informations

Latest version seen at 31.03.19, 16:42 Ok (200) 67 Byte ▾   View live available robots.

1 Click here to edit

❌ 0 mistakes ⚠ 0 mistaken items   Sending

https://www.seomarkt.de/ enter URL to test if it is blocked   Googlebot   ▾   TEST

The robots.txt tester from the Google Search Console

Present page content in a way that is understandable for Google and users alike

Good webmasters present their site equally to users and Google. When a Google Bot crawls the page, it displays the same interface as a user. Therefore, website administrators enable the Google Bot to render (predict) and index their used JavaScript, CSS and image files for the best possible performance. If, however, the robots.txt file of the respective homepage blocks the crawling of the above information, the algorithms are impaired during the rendering and indexing of the website. Webmasters therefore accept suboptimal rankings in this case. For this reason, it is worth following the advice below.

The use of a URL verification tool has proven helpful in practice. This offers the webmasters the display of the web content, which the Google Bot also gets to see. The tool can also identify and resolve any difficulties that may arise with the indexing of the website.

A clear and correct creation of the page titles increases the success of a search engine optimized page lastingly. For this process, however, the use of so-called <title> tags is indispensable. They convey a certain topic to both search engines and users. Your place is definitely within the <head> element of each page. That is why webmasters create a vivid title for both the main and sub-pages. The following figure illustrates the recommended procedure.

```
<html>
<head>
<title>BMW Car Dealership - Buy used and new cars</title>
<meta name="description=" content="The BMW dealership has a
wide range of used and new cars for sale. Additionally, it provides
buyers with numerous of financing options." >
</head>
<body>
```

Meaningful titles and snippets are indispensable for flawless search results.

On the search results page, the contents of the title tags often appear in the first line. A well-structured page title contains the title of the home page and the name of the website or company. Furthermore, users receive important information such as the company's location and the products or services offered. It is worth choosing a natural title that reflects the subject matter. Furthermore, webmasters should take great care not to select a heading that is in no way related to the content of the site. Experts recommend to avoid the use of unspecific headings like "unnamed", "divers" or "new page" and to use meaningful titles. Each page needs a title. Google is dependent on the different title names in order to read out the differences between the respective pages. Numerous companies are now also creating special websites for mobile devices. For this reason, they must also choose meaningful titles for the mobile variants of their homepage. For a successful search engine optimization, the headings of all pages of a website should differ. It is worth following the principle: "short and meaningful" with regard to the titles of the pages. Furthermore, webmasters achieve significant advantages when they provide the headlines with a certain amount of information. Long titles have not proven themselves in practice. Google displays only fractions of these or presents only an automatically generated part of a title to the user. Google reserves the right to display different titles depending on the search query made and the device selected. Another taboo for a successful title is the use of much too long title tags with useless keywords.

The meaning of the HTML snippet with the meta tag "description (HELPFULL?)".

Meta tag "descriptions" summarize the topic dealt with on one page for Google and other search engines. A page title contains either some terms or only one expression. The description meta tag of a page can have one or two sentences or whole paragraphs. The meta tag "description" is like the title tag inside the head element.

```
<html>
<head>
<title>BMW car dealer Munich - buy new car, used cars</title>
<meta name="description=" content=""BMW car dealer Munich contains
a large number of new and used BMW cars. It also offers its customers
attractive financing options.">
Insert image from metadescription" >
</head>
<body>
```

The underestimated benefits of description meta tags

Meta tags called "description" are of great importance because Google uses them as snippets when needed. However, Google also uses relevant sections of text to match users' search queries. For this reason it is worth adding "description" meta tags to the individual pages. This is particularly necessary if the search engine cannot find a high-quality text selection to display in the snippet.

Another insider tip is the correct summary of page contents. Webmasters always keep in mind the information benefit aspect when writing their description meta tags. Although there is no guideline for the length of the text, SEO experts recommend a text length that completely displays search engines. They should also score with all relevant information. On the basis of these, the users decide whether the respective page is interesting and useful for them at all. Therefore, webmasters should not use meta tags that are not related to their site. General descriptions like "This is a homepage" or "Page for car sales" are absolutely out of place and do not perform well in the Google ranking. Descriptions that only contain keywords are also bad versions of the "description" meta tags. Beginners copy the complete page content into their "description" meta tag. This approach provides neither the search engine nor the users with valuable information because it is simply too long.

Therefore a clear description of each page is worthwhile. This method helps users to retrieve the different pages within a domain. This applies in particular to searches with the site operator.

However, websites of large companies have numerous other pages. Therefore, you cannot manually label each page with "description" meta tags. In the case of a large number of pages, webmasters automatically generate the description meta tags of the respective page contents. One aspect web designers avoid is using the same description meta tags.

However, the meta-description is not directly included in the ranking as a factor, but good meta-descriptions cause users to click on them and thus contribute to an increase in the conversion rate.

Headline tags emphasize an important text

Word documents contain special header formats. These highlight an important text and tell the reader what the text is about. The same applies to the headline tags in search engine optimization. Words belonging to this category appear a little more conspicuous and larger than the traditional page text. This highlighting makes the meaning of the information reproduced clear to the reader. Webmasters can choose individual tiered sizes for their headings to create a hierarchical structure. This approach enables users to easily find their way around the document in question. Authors can imagine writing an outline. They should take a close look at the content and the associated main and subheadings of their page. So they can determine where the use of heading tags is worthwhile. However, there are also points that webmasters should avoid in order to ensure the success of their website in terms of search engine optimization. This includes, among other things, the placement of terms in heading tags which do not clearly define the interpretation of the respective page structure. Webmasters also need to know where to use headline tags. Different headline tag sizes also belong to the misplaced formats. Furthermore, the number of headings on a page should be manageable. Too many titles slay users and do not give them relevant information about what is really important. Moreover, if the number of headline tags is too high, they will not be able to recognize where the beginning and end of the topic is. The rule of thumb that long headlines do not provide meaningful content has always been valid. It can also be used wonderfully with regard to search engine optimization. Furthermore, heading tags must also make sense. The use of headings to increase the value of the design of a text is not recommnded.

Managing the display of Google search results

Web designers who practice a neat and well-structured presentation of their data benefit from numerous special functions in the search results. These include star ratings and unusual results presented. Since they play an indispensable role in search engine optimization, this book is devoted to an entire chapter of the design of the extraordinarily presented results. Search engines rely on the content of a website to crawl and index it. Therefore they also need a unique URL. The following example illustrates a URL:

```
https://hostname/path/file?requeststring#fragment
https://www.example.com/shoes/women.htm?size=7#info
```

Google recommends that web designers use the term HTTPS (https://) for all web pages. The following hostname represents the place where the homepage is hosted. As a rule, webmasters use the same name for this as they use for their e-mails. In addition, web site authors need to know that Google differentiates between pages that contain the abbreviation www. and those that are free of this designation. Persons who have decided to use the Search Console should contribute all variants. These include a page marked http://, https://, www. and a version without the abbreviation www. The other three elements such as path, file and query string determine which content of the respective server may be accessed. Additionally, upper and lower case letters play an important role in these three components. The expression "FILE" would not give the same result as the lower case "File". The host name and protocol, on the other hand, do not differentiate between the selected spelling. The last part of the URL, the fragment, which in the above example is represented by the word "Info", indicates where the browser scrolls to. Usually search engines bypass the used fragments because of the identical content. The following slashes, which are located directly after the hostname, are only a choice because they lead to the same content. The two addresses https://example.com/ and https://example.com are therefore identical.

However, if it is a file name or path, the slash below would indicate a URL that contains either another file or directory. For this reason https://example.com/womenshoes is not to be equated with https://example.com/womenshoes/.

Website designers should use simple URLs to communicate information to their readers. User-friendly URLs increase the probability that other website operators will also link to the content. Long URLs with a small number of recognizable words discourage visitors. The examples below illustrate the difference between a simple URL and an unfortunate URL.

https://www.luxury-online.com/folder3/27021984/x3/15048025.html
https://www.luxury-online.com/article/ten-rarest-earrings.html

URLs play an important role in the creation of search engine optimized texts, as they appear below the document title in the search results. Google crawls all types of URL structures, regardless of their complexity. Nevertheless, experts recommend a simple representation of the URLs. This is why URLs score points with terms that are important both for the content and for the structure of the respective homepage. They simplify the navigation on the website. For this reason, long URLs containing unnecessary parameters or even session IDs are misplaced. General page names such as "seite.html" have not proven themselves in practice. Excessive use of keywords like "schmuck-online-bestellen-onlineschmuck.html" is just as out of place as complicated URLs.

The customer is the king – this rule applies in particular to search engine optimized texts.

Copywriters who write search engine optimized articles follow some basic rules in order to achieve a high ranking position with their website. Accordingly, webmasters must put themselves in the position of their readers and ask themselves which terms users are looking for. Once you have located the informative terms, you can link them to the contents of a homepage so that users can find the page they are looking for. They distinguish between people who are familiar with the topic in question and those who still know little about the topic in question. The two groups usually do not search for the same keywords. Experienced football fans would definitely look for the term FIFA, which stands for Fédération Internationale de Football Association. Young football fans, on the other hand, would rather make a search query using the terms football final. Authors who are aware of these differences can write ideal texts for a wide target audience. With this procedure you can then enjoy numerous search results. Google AdWords has a clever keyword planner that makes your work much easier. Thanks to it, authors can find new keyword versions and inspect the possible search volume of the respective keyword more closely. In the previous chapter, the functionality and advantages of the Keyword Planner were described in detail. Furthermore, the Google Search Console displays the most popular search queries for which the respective page appears. In addition, the performance report illustrates the search queries thanks to which the majority of users have access to the respective homepage.

In the free economy, companies that find a gap in the market can survive for a long time. The same applies to search engine optimized texts. Those who offer a new type of service that cannot be found on any other website achieve comparative as well as competitive advantages. Writing a well-researched report or writing a unique story definitely adds value to a search engine optimized text. The authors can score points against the lack of experience or resources of their competitors. Thus, the creation of a search engine optimized text does not only consist in a good keyword usage, but also in finding topics that provide the user with a high added value, but are not yet present on the Internet. Authors who regularly produce texts know that they must be understandable and comprehensible for readers. These two conditions also apply to SEO texts. Unprofessional articles with spelling and grammar mistakes not only scare off readers, but also damage the company's image. Linguistic and syntactic errors are absolutely taboo, since they do not lend a serious touch to the respective enterprise side. Search engine optimized texts must strive for perfection, as they represent the offered products, services as well as the company to the outside world. In today's highly networked world, online texts often establish the first contact between a customer and the respective organization. Therefore also embarrassing as well as badly represented contents are undesirable. Good texts impress with a clear structure and informative subheadings. Experienced authors avoid useless copying of existing content. Web designers are best at producing good texts if they always keep in mind to design them optimally for their readers in the first place. Nevertheless, search engine optimized articles are texts that are also aimed at being found by the search engines and considered useful. However, the type of content the site has to offer is irrelevant to Google. Texts about products, services, press releases or content marketing content must be written in such a way that a search engine can easily understand them. This is the only way it is able to place the page high up in the rankings. This is because SEO texts form a symbiosis with the keywords and practically cannot exist without each other. SEO texts that do not contain keywords do not belong to the search engine optimized text group. Unfortunately, for this reason, a minority of authors still believe that they have to spam texts with their keywords in order to deliver a search engine optimized article. Therefore, writers who understand the term keyword density achieve higher success with their texts than their competitors who do keyword spamming. Keyword Density is the English term for the term keyword density. This stands for the relative concept of writing texts with a keyword density of five percent. This procedure does not provide any meaningful content. That is why the WDF*IDF formula came into being in 2012. This is used to calculate how a certain text behaves in comparison to the competing texts. The formula takes the keyword density into account and searches for other keywords that belong to the written text according to the formula. Termslabs.io and Content Succes are the names of the tools that help authors to use the WDF formula. The WDF*IDF analysis helps authors find meaningful words for their SEO text. The tool helps companies to achieve comparative competitive advantages and set a unique selling proposition. In this way, clever authors of website content filter out keywords that occur relatively often in a text on the subject of "dietary supplements", for example, but are not represented in all web texts. The connective word "or" very often appears in articles on the subject of dietary supplements, but also in all texts of the competition. Terms such as "harmful to health", "inexpensive" and "efficient" appear in the same sense in only one presentation reporting on dietary supplements.

Authors usually use the WDF*IDF tool to search for meaningful keywords. A good keyword rate lies in the use of these terms in every section of a text and, if the context permits, also in the headings. Talkative copywriters use synonyms to loosen up their articles. However, they deliberately refrain from an obsessive and frequent use of keywords. Good copywriters also pay attention to grammatical adjustments. Furthermore, they are not afraid of using necessary filler words or prepositions, as an appealing writing style with a high user-friendliness is still in the foreground.

Structure of a meaningful SEO text

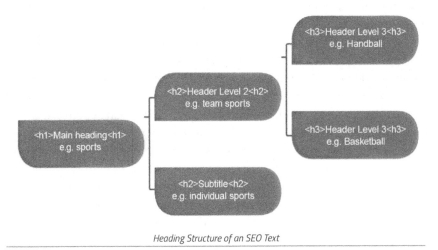

Heading Structure of an SEO Text

Sensible SEO texts enable their readers to quickly fly over the content, from which they can read all important information. Headings represent the core content of a paragraph. Nevertheless, the type of text dominates.

Product descriptions, testimonials, press releases and a company history are not subject to the same style of writing, although they have some similarities. This includes, among other things, the structure of a logical header structure. The main heading is provided with the HTML code h1. This is followed by further headings with the award h2. In the event that further headings are required within this section, these must be marked via h3. Headings play an important role in well optimized SEO texts. They help both the users and the search engines to quickly classify the displayed content to a topic area. For this reason, search engine-optimized texts also contain meaningfully embedded keywords in their headings. However, when choosing a heading that contains a keyword and a meaningful title that is keyword-free, experts recommend that you choose the second variant.

Optimally structured texts consist of several paragraphs. This makes the article many times easier to read. Jump marks are among the other necessary elements that a search engine optimized text contains. These are expressed in the form of fold-out illustrations. They enjoy great popularity among readers because they still provide them with a perfect overview of the content.

They also enable users to navigate much faster through the website. Mobile users are dependent on this property. However, the essential content should not remain hidden on the desktop.

Fonts should be able to be presented by everyday browsers. In addition, the selected font should be easy for the user to read. Many authors do not know how long their text should be. The rule of thumb: A good text should be as long as necessary, but as short as possible. The competition can serve as a helpful orientation. Expansions with unnecessary filler words deter users. Quality definitely takes precedence over quantity with regard to the length of an SEO text. The following five basic rules can be used by copywriters as an orientation for writing a search engine optimized text.

1 Determine the target audience and construct a structured content

The definition of the target group that copywriters want to reach with their formulations has priority. Thus the question of the desired target group represents the beginning of a good SEO text. A look at the actions of the competition can also provide helpful information. Journalists follow the W-question principle before writing a press release. Authors who want to write down successful search engine optimized formulation scan also acquire this technique. The first question is: Who plays the leading role in my SEO text? These can be products, services or people. Secondly, the answer to the question of what plays an important role. It is all about what the product or service offers. Third is the question of location. Here the authors answer where readers can purchase the offer. However, in the case of a report on a person or an event, the 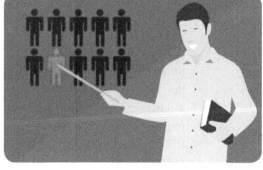 authors also address the location of the event. In addition, readers want to know when they can purchase their desired object. That is why conscientious copywriters do not leave out the question of the time. The clarification of how something works or how a certain event took place also belongs in a search engine optimized text. Also the question of why the product offers an additional benefit is not ignored by the authors. The same applies to press releases. The readers want to be informed about the reason of an event. Due to the fact that this should not be known, the subscribers are also happy about speculation. In the Internet age, the origin of information plays an important role. That is why experienced and good copywriters always refer to their sources. Those who adhere to the rules mentioned make a great contribution to the success of a perfect search engine optimized text.

Good texts captivate with their unique contents and the same applies to search engine optimized formulations. However, many authors misunderstand these challenges and try to reinvent the wheel. All you need to do is hold up your personal Unique-Selling-Point (USP). In addition, the associated information should be presented more extensively than that of the competition. The copy and paste approach is definitely not desirable. Instead, texts that are characterized by authenticity score points. While authors always focus on their target audience, they are careful not to outsource other potential readers. As a rule, search engine optimized texts do not contain regional dialects, as the inhabitants outside the respective region have to struggle with comprehension problems.

Those who have dealt with the topic of duplicate content know very well why unique copies are important. Since a duplicated content considerably reduces the success rate, this topic will be discussed in detail at this point. It should act as a protection against the writing of an already similar content. The duplicated content is a web page content that already exists on the Internet in this or a similar way. As a rule, there is no intent of deception behind this. A duplicated content that was not intentionally created includes discussion forums that create regular and shortened pages on mobile devices. Stock items that are referenced via numerous tangible URLs also belong in the category of unknowingly duplicated content. Many users also do not know that print versions of web pages are also part of a duplicate. If a domain contains multiple pages with identical content, webmasters can use different methods to tell Google their preferred URL. Canonization is the technical term for this procedure. From time to time, copywriters deliberately produce content that is then duplicated on different websites. In this way, you pursue the goal of improving your ranking with the search engines. Such methods never go down well with the users.

They get angry about search results that give them the same content. For this reason, Google aims to present pages with different information content. A suitable filter ensures that only one page is displayed if a normal and a print version are available. In cases where Google has deliberate intent to deceive, an index and ranking correction will be made to the relevant website. Webmasters must then expect a lower rating for their website. In the worst case, a removal from the Google index takes place. If this is the case, the page will no longer appear in the search results. For the mentioned reasons it is worthwhile to create unique copies. Numerous activities can help to avoid duplicates.

✓ Experienced webmasters rely on top-level domains. This allows Google to provide the right variant of a document to produce the desired country-specific content. A website as in the previous example www.furniture.de stands for country-specific content for Germany. The domain www.furniture.com/de or de.furniture.com is not as unique as the first example.

✓ Careful unification of the content prevents duplicates from occurring. Administrators must ensure that Google considers the same version as the site operators to be preferred. For this reason, all websites on which the content is standardized should contain a link to the original article.

✓ The Search Console can be used as a helpful tool in communicating the wishes regarding the indexing of the website. Google receives information about the preferred domain. In the above example this would be http://www.furniture.de or http://furniture.de

✓ Minimizing repeated text sections is also part of the avoidance strategies of annoying duplicates. It is not worth pointing out long copyrights at the end of every subpage. Instead, a brief summary with an integrated link containing detailed information on this topic is sufficient.

✓ Placeholders have a negative effect when producing a unique content. Page visitors find empty pages annoying. Therefore, clever webmasters do not publish pages for which they have not yet produced suitable content. Those who cannot work without the placeholder pages should avoid indexing these empty pages by using the meta tag "noindex".

- ✓ Careful analysis of the content management systems used is another aspect that effectively counteracts duplicates. It is worth checking how the content is presented on the website. Forums, blogs and other similar systems often display the same content in different formats. Individual blog entries can appear on the homepage of a blog and on a website with different entries.
- ✓ Minimizing similar content is one of the safe ways to avoid duplicates. Travel agencies that have two websites about a city should merge them into a single page.

Experts also recommend blocking crawler access to duplicates using the robots.txt file. Search engines cannot determine whether web pages present the same content if they do not crawl it. They treat them as separate pages, although this is not the case. For this reason, website owners recommend that search engines be allowed to crawl URLs, but mark them as duplicate using the rel="canonical" link element, the URL parameter tool, or the 301 redirects. When Google crawls a powerful section of the website, webmasters can adjust the settings called "crawling frequency" in the Search Console.

- ✓ However, duplicate content does not mean that webmasters will have to reckon with penalties unless they knowingly produced it to manipulate users and search results.
- ✓ If Google's controls determine that a planned attempt at deception has been made, and for this reason does not display the page in the results, web site operators can refer to the webmaster's detailed guidelines on how to proceed to make the duplicate content unique. After a successful review and to ensure that the requirements have been met, webmasters can send a request for a re-audit of their website.
- ✓ In exceptional cases, the algorithm selects the domain of an exter nal homepage on which the content is hosted without the consent of the webmaster. Those who believe that the copyright law has been violated may contact the host of the respective site and request that the content be removed. Furthermore, they should request the removal of the website that infringes the copyrights from the search engine results in Google. This should comply with US copyright law.

❷ Select keywords carefully and use them sparingly

The subject of keywords has already been explained. The following guideline serves a professional ON-Page optimization. Webmasters who follow these rules benefit from a higher ranking of their website. The agency SEO-Markt GmbH has applied this approach in practice and thus helped its clients to a higher success of their website.

Guide to Professional OnPage Optimization (Competitive)

Without a good ON-Page optimization webmasters can assume that they will not be found on Google or other search engines. This guide provides valuable tips and tricks on how to launch your website into the top position of all search engines. In addition, optimization measures such as a good image caption are also explained, since these are important for a good ranking position, but are still underestimated in practice. Those who implement the following advice are definitely a step ahead of their competitors. To a successful ON-Page optimization also a successful URL belongs, this is also discussed in the following.

❶ Permalink

Good webmasters pay attention to an optimal permalink. This is a composition of the terms permanent and hyperlink. It is therefore a permanent link that is present on the Internet. Permalinks serve as important tools in search engine optimization. In practice, voice URLs have proven to be both user and search engine friendly. However, webmasters should be careful to choose a permalink that is as short as possible. It would also be advantageous if it contains the keyword, since the rule "The closer the keyword is to the main domain, the more relevant it is evaluated" applies. www. dogfood.com/permalink is an example of a permalink that you can apply to your website.

❷ Title Tag / meta Title resp. Page Title

The Title Tag, whose German translation is website title, is one of Google's more than 500 ranking factors. For this reason he deserves special attention. It serves as the title of your own page in the search results.

Preview metadata

The Title Tag, whose German translation is website title, is one of Google's more than 500 ranking factors. For this reason he deserves special attention. It serves as the title of your own page in the search results. However, webmasters should always keep in mind that this should not exceed the length of 70 characters. Furthermore, you should not forget that the title tag plays a major role in a careful ON-Page optimization. If web designers neglect this, they can assume that they will be defeated by their competitors. Title tags in combination with the meta-description represent the first points of contact between the user and the respective website. If you carefully match these two components, you can significantly increase your click rate and gain more visitors in organic search with this approach. When creating your title, webmasters should consider the following four key points:

✓ Without spaces, the maximum length of the title is 70 characters.
✓ Good titles offer users added value and encourage them to visit your website.
✓ Each individual URL has a title.
✓ Furthermore, the main keyword is in the title, if possible even at the beginning.

The example "Buying dresses for ladies online Otto" contains only 31 characters and provides the user with all the information he needs. Furthermore, putting the brand or domain name in the title is a good strategy that has proven successful in practice. That is why this is a perfect title.

❸ Meta description

If the search engines do not find a good text selection to display in a snippet, it is worth adding "description" meta tags. These score points with their additional information value. According to experts, the text should be long enough to be displayed in full. Because the users decide on the basis of these texts whether they want to read the article or not. This is a short description of the respective page. Even if the meta-description does not flow directly into the ranking, it still causes users to click on it frequently. Experienced authors take a look at the competition and orient themselves on its meta-descriptions. They try to eliminate the weak points of their competitors and thus to overthrow the competition from the top position with Google. For this reason, webmasters should carefully select the "meta-description" and take into account the advice given. Webmasters can use the free SERP snippet generator to optimize their title. Thanks to it, they can also perform the meta-description. An example of a tool is: serpsim.com.

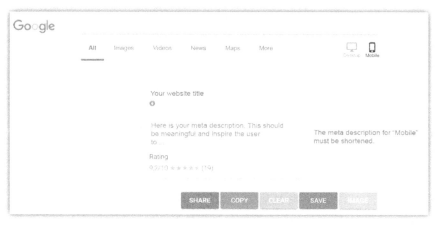

Preview metadata on mobile devices

4 Headings (Heading Tags): (including integration of keywords)

Headings play an important role in the structure of documents. They require logical and hierarchical use. Since time is a scarce commodity in today's fast-moving world, the majority of readers skim a text. In addition, a large part of the text is based on the headings and then decides whether the text is useful or not. In this way, users can better assess the content. The clever Google Bot does the same. In a hierarchical representation of headings, only one main heading exists. The following example serves as an illustration.

```
<h1> Header that contains the main topic of the document </h1>
<h2> Introduction of the text </h2>
<h2> Disadvantages </h2>
<h3> A disadvantage viewed in detail </h3>
<h2> Fulness </h2>
```

Authors should be careful to include the relevant keyword in the headings. Webmasters should always keep in mind that the title of an article is also the page title of the document. Many users have difficulty finding the right headline because they think in SEO titles instead of putting themselves in the position of their readers. Experts recommend that authors consider the following five points when finding a suitable heading.

1. A good heading is short and concise and consists of five or fewer terms.
2. It offers the reader a high information content.
3. In addition, the keyword makes the beginning of a successful heading.
4. The headline is clear and the reader knows what the article is about without having read the full text.
5. The expectations of readers. With regard to finding a successful heading, a comparison with the competition is recommended.

⑤ Text / Content

Good search engine optimized texts are a must for a successful ON-Page optimization. The rules of the journalists can provide a great remedy. The seven W questions already explained serve as valuable guidelines for successful text creation. Another important aspect that should not be neglected is the creation of a unique content. Furthermore, search engine optimized texts are written in such a way that both the target group and those who do not belong to it feel that they have been picked up. In addition, the texts should be continuously updated. Those who are not sure how long their article should be can take a look at the competition and determine the ideal word count (Competitive Intelligence). Experts definitely recommend a comparison with the top ten sites of the competition.

⑥ Images and ALT attributes

An ALT attribute stands for the description of a text. The abbreviation "ALT" symbolizes the term alternative. Image files located on Web pages contain the ALT attribute. If the image cannot be displayed, the ALT text appears instead. Thanks to this attribute, search engines can better recognize the image content. Data maintenance of this attribute is therefore worthwhile. Visually impaired users in particular benefit from this attribute because they can have the text read aloud. In practice, an ALT attribute looks like this:

```
<img src="directory/image.jpg" alt="This is
an informative image description">
```

Webmasters can use this example to label their images, especially for visually impaired people. You should definitely take this step, because in practice there are still many reasons why images are not displayed. This is partly due to defective image files or defective links. Also the activated tracking protection of many browsers often prevents a correct display of an image. The browser named Mozilla offers its users the possibility to deliberately hide the display of images. In addition, broken URLs are also to blame if a graphic or image is not displayed.

The reason for this is the renaming or moving of the respective server. The reason why this section of the chapter is devoted to ALT attributes is because of their importance for users and search engine optimization. ALT tags provide search engines with important information about the image content as well as the entire content of the website. For this reason, webmasters need to optimize their ALT tags. You should also include the main keyword in your ALT tag. This significantly improves the focus of the respective keyword. However, web designers should avoid spamming the keyword as much as possible. Furthermore, they should be aware of the keywords in the ALT tags to improve their position in the ranking. For this reason, the optimization of ALT attributes is part of a holistic SEO. The following example illustrates this situation and can also serve as a guide.

An operator of an informative blog about dogs uses a special picture of a four-legged friend in his contribution. In this example the URL of the page is: mydog.de/dogs-with-short-fur. Accordingly, the integration of the image should read as follows:

```
<img src="/dogs-with-short-fur.jpg" alt="Young Rottweiler
puppy black with very short and black fur">
```

If webmasters pay attention to a cooperation of the file name with the keyword, they can strengthen the content of the respective URL. Nevertheless, text writers should take the size of the respective file into consideration when optimizing the images. This is due to the high importance for the loading time and the performance of the respective website.

7 **Internal links**

Internal links occupy an important place in the Google algorithm ranking. They are also the secret for success. They are characterized by numerous notable advantages. With regard to the number, placement and design of the respective link texts, webmasters can proceed as they wish. However, they should take note of the information that links that are frequently clicked on are among the good variants. Usually these are links, which:

✓ are in the area of the content
✓ that can be found at the beginning of a text

- ✓ are recognized by the users as a link (they are either highlighted or underlined)
- ✓ are characterized by a direct connection to the respective text
- ✓ are placed on a page that enjoys a high number of visitors
- ✓ compete with a small number of other links.

⑧ Pagespeed

Pagespeed will be covered in detail in the next chapter.

2.6

PAGESPEED - THE MOST IMPORTANT FACTOR?

Pagespeed stands for the duration of the speed required to load the content of a page. However, many users confuse the terms Page Speed and Site Speed. Experts define them either as "page load time" or as "time to first byte". The former stands as "time until the complete presentation of a selected page content", the latter however for the "time until the browser receives the first byte". Webmasters evaluate their page speed using Google PageSpeed Insights. The speed score of the mentioned PageSpeed Insights contains valuable data from the Chrome User Experience Report (CruX). It also contains further reports on two important speed metrics. They consist of the "First Contentful Paint" (FCP) and the DOMContentLoaded (DCL).

PageSpeed Insights: https://developers.google.com/speed/pagespeed/insights/

Suggestions for a successful search engine optimization in combination with the Page Speed

Google uses the page speed as a signal for the evaluation of the respective page algorithm. Analyses have proven that Google apparently accurately measures the time to the first byte when considering page speed. Accordingly, a slow website speed has negative consequences for the website operator. Search engines can therefore crawl considerably fewer pages with their allocated "thinning budget". However, this has a negative impact on indexation. Moreover, page speed is not only important for Google, but also for the user experience. In today's fast-paced world, speed is an important attribute that website operators have to take into account in search engine optimization in order to assert themselves against the competition. This is because users usually expect fully loaded content within three seconds. They also assume a rapid charging time in the case of a poor mobile phone connection. Google also includes the loading time of a page in the page ranking. Websites that are characterized by a long loading time also accept high bounce rates as well as a short dwell time of their visitors. Furthermore, longer loading times have a negative effect on conversions. To counteract the high bounce rate and short dwell time, experts have formulated valuable advice to help website operators increase their page speed. These are explained below.

Before webmasters start work, they should first open the following page **https://developers.google.com/speed/pagespeed/insights/** and then analyze their own website. Google then presents tips and instructions on how to improve website speed.

❶   Activate Compression

Gzip has proven to be a helpful software application for file compression. It can reduce the size of CSS, HTML and JavaScript files if they are larger than 150 bytes. However, Gzip is not suitable for compressing image files. For this the site operators need Photoshop which is they are obliged to pay the costs.

❷   CSS, JavaScript and HTML reduce

Experts advise website operators to optimize their code, as this measure can increase their page speed many times over. It is worth removing spaces, commas and other unnecessary characters. Code comments, formatting and unused code are also unnecessary and increase page speed. For this reason, Google recommends the use of CSSNano and UdlifyJS.

③ **Minimize the number of redirects**

Redirects are a popular element that web designers use to bring the entire content to their visitors, but they also require additional time. When users are directed to another page, they need to complete the HTTP request response cycle.

④ **Removing the JavaScripts**

To render a page, browsers must create a DOM tree using HTML analysis. If a browser encounters a script at the time of this process, it must be slowed down and executed before a continuation can take place. Accordingly, Google recommends to minimize the blocking of the JavaScript and if possible to avoid it altogether.

⑤ **Using Browser Caching**

Browsers have the ability to store a lot of information, such as stylesheets, images, or JavaScript files, so they don't have to reload the page when a user returns to their page. For this reason it is worth using the tool called YSlow. Web designers can use it to check whether an expiration date has been set for their cache.

⑥ **Improve server response time**

The response time of a server depends on several factors. These include the number of data traffic received by users, the resources accessed by the site, the software used by the server, and the hosting solution. In order to optimize the response time of the server, it is worthwhile to rectify faults. These include slow database queries, slow routing, or lack of memory. The best response time of the server is less than 200 milliseconds.

⑦ **Use a network to distribute content**

Content Distribution Networks (CDNs) or Content Delivery Networks are networks of servers that distribute content. As a rule, copies of a website are stored in different local computer centers. Accordingly, users can access the target page faster and more securely.

⑧ Optimize images

Webmasters should pay strict attention to a suitable image optimization, as this has a strong effect on the page speed. They should therefore be the right size. PNG file formats are more suitable for graphics whose number of colors is less than 16. Whereas the JPEG format should be chosen for the representation of photos. Good images are also compressed for the web. For this reason, it is worth using CSS sprites to create good image templates. This is particularly recommended for pictures that appear frequently on the website. Buttons as well as symbols are characterized by a frequent appearance on the web page. CSS Sprites is a clever solution because they combine the selected images into one large image. Charging takes place at the same time. Accordingly, a smaller number of HTTP requests is required. In addition, only the required sections are displayed. This is a smart way to save loading time so users don't have to wait for a lot of pictures to load.

Mobile First Indexing and its importance for users of Smartphones

As the number of smartphone users continues to grow, Google search also shows a higher increase on mobile devices. Nevertheless, the ranking systems still determine the relevance of the pages using the desktop versions. However, this causes difficulties because the mobile page versions have a smaller amount of content than the conventional variants of the homepages. For this reason, the algorithms are not 100 percent capable of analyzing the pages that the users of the mobile devices actually see. In order to close this gap, search engine experts have started testing the targeted conversion to a so-called Mobile First index. This is an index which distinguishes mobile versions of websites. It is believed that in the future there will only be one search index consisting of websites and apps. The algorithms will mainly be based on the mobile page versions in order to determine the page ranking, to collect ordered data and to present the snippets of the respective homepages in the search results. Even if the index consists of mobile documents, all users will continue to benefit from an excellent search experience. This applies to both the mobile and desktop versions.

Responsible developers have approached this conversion process with extreme caution. To this end, they carried out a small number of tests in order to carry out a major changeover afterwards. They have proceeded in such a way as to spare users from any search restrictions. Webmasters who maintain a responsive website or homepage with a dynamic delivery where the most important content and markup are identical in the desktop and mobile variants do not need to adapt anything.

If the content and the markup of the desktop and mobile variants differ in significant points in the website configuration, it is worth making some changes to the homepage. First, the site operators should provide a structured markup for both versions. Managers can test the equivalence of the variants by entering the URLs of both options into the intended test tool for systematically structured data. They shall then compare the results supplied. Webmasters should not use a comprehensive markup that is irrelevant to the specific information content of the temporary document when providing the structured data for the mobile website. The robots-txt tester allows to check the mobile version of the respective page in the Google Bot. It should be possible to find it there. Changes to the canonical links are unnecessary. They will continue to be used to show users the desired results when searching on their desktop and mobile devices.

Web page operators who have only made the desktop version of their page in the Search Console can easily add the mobile version and make a confirmation. Those who only provide a desktop page can assume that the search engines index it easily, even if the users access it with a mobile device.

Those who are in the process of creating a mobile version of their homepage should strictly consider constructing it error-free and complete. That is why it is worth completing a flawless desktop version and then creating a mobile version when the former is complete.

Display and instructions for creating Accelerated Mobile Pages

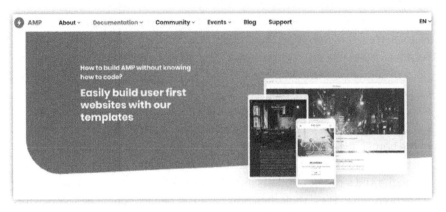

On the website www.amp.devyou will find valuable resources

Mobile pages should have another characteristic besides a friendly operability. This results in a fast loading time of the mobile version of the site. If this leaves something to be desired, the number of page visitors who leave the website increases. For this reason, not only does mobile page optimization function as an important side of the medal, but the speed of the mobile website also functions as the other side of the coin. The technical term that encourages users to take a closer look at the content presented is accelerated mobile pages (AMP). A clarification of this fact in figures, proves that with a loading time, which exceeds the 3-second limit, enterprises must accept heavy losses in turnover. Google has found that AMP can reduce the loading time of a page between 15 and 85 percent. As early as 2015, Google announced that accelerated mobile pages could become an important ranking factor. For this reason, SEO consultants, webmasters and marketers have taken a closer look at AMP and found that it has a significant impact on the ranking of search results. Accordingly, AMP-optimized pages benefit not only from better placement, but also from the ability to convert page visitors into customers.

The Meaning of Accelerated Mobile Pages (AMP)

The origin of AMP lies in Google and Twitter. Successful site operators integrate AMP as part of a mobile content strategy. This procedure loads a page more quickly using a decomposition. AMP is thus also a proof that puts its users in the focus of the action. Accelerated Mobile Pages is an open source platform that aims to help web designers optimize their mobile content for speed and readability. After all, faster mobile websites with readable content provide a better user experience.

How AMP works

AMP is able to process mobile data much faster by reducing HTML tags or using only those that are best suited for the respective mobile user. Accordingly, AMP uses an optimized HTML for the processing of a page. The goal is a faster page load time. Accordingly, HTML tags, which significantly slow down the speed of the website, are eliminated. Integrated JavaScripts prevent the use of the script for the Accelerated Mobile Pages. To benefit from the advantages of AMP, webmasters use an optimized CSS version.

- ✓ Web designers may only use the JavaScript library provided by AMP. The loading time can be a little longer, as the site operators have no control over the library provided.
- ✓ A correct validation of the pages is necessary in order to guarantee a perfect function of the web pages.
- ✓ The AMP pages do not allow the use of forms.
- ✓ Individual fonts require an extra charge in order to offer the site visitor a more enjoyable user experience.
- ✓ In illustrations, it is essential to indicate the height and width, otherwise they look strange.
- ✓ Those who want to integrate videos into their pages should use AMP-supported extensions.

Webmasters who use AMP to improve their mobile site versions should put speed and readability before divisibility. The Social Share buttons are not displayed correctly every time because the majority of them were created with JavaScript.

Significant advantages of Accelerated Mobile Pages (AMP)

There is a significant correlation between page speed, page views and search engine rankings. Page administrators should always keep in mind that website visitors click their way through multiple sub-pages, and that for this reason the bounce rate is reduced when the page loads quickly. A low bounce rate and a good onsite experience will be rewarded by Google. AMP Web Sites are ranked higher than Web Sites that do not take advantage of AMP.

❶ Fast web pages that visitors love

Speed is the focus of a mobile website. Good content is necessary, but is not noticed by the visitors when the page loads slowly. Studies have shown that even a 1-second delay in mobile loading time increases the conversion rate by 3.5 percent, page views by 9.4 percent and the dreaded bounce rate by 8.3 percent. For this reason, speed is the focus of attention. Slow mobile pages cannot convert the desired target group to customers. That is why the site called AMPProject.org helps with the optimization.

❷ Improved visibility for content marketers

Google now also displays AMP results in organic search results. These can be identified by the AMP icon in green. The principle is simple: the more attention the search results receive, the more clicks they receive. The green AMP symbol improves the click-through rate, as the search results differ many times over from the results of the competition. Users search specifically for AMP websites because they are informed about their faster loading time.

❸ Better search engine rankings

The connection between the speed of the mobile website and the conversion rate deserves special attention. If website visitors are happy with the fast-loading version of the site, they are more likely to buy and subscribe to a product or service. Mobile websites enjoy a higher status in organic search results. Accordingly, AMP-based pages are more likely to gain an even higher ranking.

④ Adaptable display help

The majority of people create a website or a blog in order to earn something on the side or even to change their profession. With AMP, however, they can earn money on their mobile websites with the help of ads. This is because not all HTML tags are executed, but only an optimized CSS version is used. Since no JavaScripts are used, the coding is easier. Furthermore, webmasters should keep in mind that third party ads on their Acclerated Mobile Pages should load quickly in order to attract the attention of site visitors and thus achieve comparative competitive advantages. Content marketing is an effective way to increase impact, help website visitors answer questions, and optimize the return on investment of advertising costs. Among the ad networks that have proven themselves in practice and that use the functionality of AMP ads are Amazon A9, AdReactor, Google Doubleclick, Flite, Adform, Google AdSense, AOL AdTech, DotAndAds.

⑤ Simplified user tracking

A traffic line to the mobile side is just the beginning. Webmasters have to verify whether their visitors have actually arrived at their site. Tracking is an effective tool for tracking the origin of website visitors. Thanks to AMP it is much easier to track both the users and the performance of the site. Analytical tools allow an accurate inspection of the selected AMP version. After all, website operators can only influence the behavior of their visitors if they have the opportunity to understand it. AMP provides the webmaster with two different tags. They help track essential data such as conversions, videos, link tracking, traffic, and differentiate between new and returning users. Well-known companies that take advantage of AMP include WordPress, Adobe Analytics, Pinterest, Twitter and LinkedIn.

Page optimization for AMP

Accelerated Mobile Pages is still in the development phase. Accordingly, regular updates will appear. However, website operators need to optimize their pages for AMP. They have various options at their disposal for this purpose. Beginners should have two page variants for security reasons. The first version is the original page of the mobile-friendly version. Accordingly, the second page is the AMP version of the special web page, which serves to speed up the process. Furthermore, webmasters should always keep in mind that the AMP page is based on HTML and therefore does not allow formatting elements or JavaScripts from third parties. Also leaving user comments is currently not possible with AMP versions. The focus of the AMP versions is on the attributes readability and speed.

Step-by-Step Guide for WordPress

1. WordPress users must first download the WordPress plugin "AMP" to start using AMP. The AMP plugin can be easily installed in the WordPress Dashboard.
2. After a successful installation and activation, webmasters must add "/amp/" to their respective blog entry. Those who don't have a permalink can enter "?amp=1" as an alternative instead. Users must be able to understand the AMP scheme. For example, if the canonical page is the example url.de/ladies' clothing, then the link to the AMP version should be amp.diebeispielurl.de/ladies' clothing or the example url.de/ladies' clothing and test.de/ladies' clothing. When website visitors click on the link to the respective AMP page via Google search, the AMP URL appears in the browser. To prevent confusion among users, webmasters must ensure that the AMP URL matches their site.
3. They then confirm and optimize this entry in the Google Search Console. This allows you to select your AMP version more quickly.

Those who cannot use WordPress should check whether a suitable AMP plugin exists for their CMS. If no plugin is available, the web designers won't get any further without any knowledge of HTML. However, you can follow the instructions below to create a suitable AMP version for your website:

```
https://amp.dev/documentation/guides-and-tutorials/
start/create/?format=websites
```

Conclusion

AMP is an effective upgrade for mobile-friendly websites that helps webmasters accelerate their page content. They also meet Google's requirements by using AMP. Experts believe that Accelerated Mobile Pages will have a strong impact on social media interactions.

 Tip:

To create a new website, you can download ready-made AMP templates from https://amp.dev/documentation/templates

2.7

THE POWER OF STRUCTURED DATA

Structured data do an enormous amount of groundwork for the Google Bot. They provide him with further information which Google can use to classify the pages more optimally and thus display them more accurately for certain search queries. Below is some advice on using rich snippets, rich cards, featured snippets, and the Google Knowledge Graph.

A markup helps to add well-structured data

Structured data is a handy code that webmasters can add to each page of their website. They serve the better illustration of the side contents for search machines. These in turn make use of the data provided in order to present the contents as well as possible and conspicuously as possible. This increases the probability that exactly the right customers will find the respective product or service offered by a company. Cosmetics manufacturers who operate an online shop and equip their product pages with the aforementioned markup benefit from better information provision with the search engines. They then see that the respective page contains information about the decorative cosmetics, their prices and helpful feedback from customers. When users make meaningful searches, they can expect to find them in the search results snippet. In this case, experts speak of so-called rich search results.

However, structured data markups are not only suitable for rich search results, but also for essential results that can be displayed in other formats. Medical practices benefit from the markup of opening hours because they are found by their patients exactly when they are dependent on them. The persons also see whether the practice is open or closed at the time of the search. There are some elements that webmasters should mark up in order to increase the success of their companies. For suppliers of products, the markup equipment of the products is worthwhile. The company logo, company location and opening hours are among the terms that should be provided with a markup. Important markup elements also include lists of events and dates, the company logo, recipes and videos about the products and services offered. Webmasters who are familiar with this topic recommend to support all relevant contents of the structured data with a markup. An HTML code helps with this presentation. However, there are also two tools called Highlighter and Markup-Help, which can help you with the desired presentation of the structured data.

For optimal results, web designers should verify their used markup with a test for rich search results. In this way, you can check whether the implementation you have performed does not contain any errors. They either enter the URL or copy the HTML code that contains the markup. However, there are some rules that web designers should avoid if they attach great importance to successful search engine optimization. This includes, among other things, the use of invalid markups or so-called data highlighters. The latter allow a structured markup without changing the source code of the website. This is a free tool provided by the Search Console. Those who want to prepare the markup code for duplication and insertion on their site can use the Markup Help. However, web designers should not change their source code if they are unsure about implementing a markup.

In the Search Console there are helpful reports about improvements of the website. They indicate the number of pages detected by a particular markup on the Web page. The reports also show the frequency with which pages appear in search results and the number of users who have visited the site in the last three months. Furthermore, Google lists the detected errors in the reports mentioned above. However, web designers should not add markup data that the user cannot see. It is also not advisable to make false valuations.

The importance of structured data

Structured data provides website content with useful additional information. Google Bots understand the content of the pages better thanks to them. Webmasters can also use structured data to present their content as rich snippets in Google search results. This makes them stand out clearly from the other results and they enjoy greater attention. This in turn increases the click rate and the number of visitors. The following chapter explains the various display options that can be implemented with the help of structured data. Webmasters who use them can enjoy their web page display in the search results.

How to create rich snippets

Rich snippets are immediately noticed by website visitors. The challenge is to generate them for your own website. Markups are the basis for this realization. These are awards in the source code. However, these have no effect on the browser display. They are made up of two parts. The first component of a source code, for example, is an event. The second component is the properties, i.e. the properties such as the date. The two components are called schemata. Further marking types are Microdata, RDFa and JSON-LD. The first two use webmasters for attributes. You describe existing elements in the HTML body of a page. Whereas JSON-LD is added to the HTML

header of a page without complicated measures in presented structures. Google allows all formats, but the search engine prefers JSON-LD. Webmasters who want to display snippets as rich snippets can use four methods depending on their IT skills and backend access.

❶   Manual implementation

With this procedure, which is carried out in the source code, webmasters use the schema.org page to select the appropriate coding. It is available there for all property types in the required three formats. The markup is implemented at the appropriate point in the source code.

❷   Use plugins for implementation

Meanwhile, extensions and plug-ins exist for all content management systems such as WordPress. These make it easier for webmasters to implement their structured data. Thanks to this, website operators do not have to change or edit the source code on their own. The Mark-Up plugin called JSON-LD is the most popular for the content management system for WordPress. At Joomla! the Google Structured Data Markup is very popular.

❸ Implementation using the Google Tag Manager

For those who want to implement without an IT department, JSON-LD can also be added via Google Tag Manager. First they create the JSON-LD markup and insert it with the custom HTML tag into the tag manager. Triggers then help to link to the appropriate subpage.

❹ Implementation using the Data Highlighter

Google's Data Highlighter is the most convenient way to structure data. This is especially worthwhile if the webmasters do not have access to the backend of their website. At product pages, webmasters train Google to filter out important information such as price, color or manufacturing material within a very short time. This information is then automatically identified on websites with the same structure.

Google Data Highlighter: https://www.google. com/webmasters/tools/data-highlighter

It plays a subordinate role which of the implementation types mentioned webmasters choose. You should also know that you do not have to fill out all the markup types that are available. Each Mark-Up contains mandatory and voluntary fields.

Testing Structured Data Successfully

After a successful implementation of the markup, the success is checked. This task can be performed with the Structured Data Testing Tool. Website designers check whether the markup contains any discrepancies. The tool scores with its easy handling. Webmasters can use it to test both a URL and a code.

Test tool for structured data: https://search.google.com/structured-data/testing-tool/

Definition of Rich Cards

Rich Cards serve as an extension of the Rich Snippets. But they show significant differences to these.

✓ Rich Cards are only suitable for mobile searches. Users can click through different results with the help of a picture carousel.

✓ Currently, rich cards exist for a small number of types. These include films, recipes, articles and courses. However, feverish efforts are being made to develop further types.

✓ The hallmark of the Rich Cards are large images with a small text.

How to create Rich Cards

Rich Cards are based on markups which are based on the Microdata, RDFa or JSON-LD format. Webmasters can therefore fall back on the four implementation options already described. The Structured Data Testing Tool mentioned above can also be used with regard to Rich Cards. There is even a report for this in the Google Search Console. This provides valuable feedback on how Rich Cards are played for your own online presence. In this way, webmasters can look up their discrepancies and potential for improvement in a targeted men.

Definition of the Google Knowledge Graph Panel

The Knowledge Graph Panel is the third alternative. It stands for a determination of compiled search results for selected topics and entities. It is usually used for knowledge or company-related search queries. Knowledge-related questions include the search terms "artificial intelligence" or "Salvador Dali". The company-related inquiries consist of two parts. On the one hand they deliver brand results like Nike and on the other hand they display store opening hours like adidas-store. The user receives local search results if he has searched for a store near him. Companies that aim to appear as a web page within the Knowledge Graph Panel in search results can pursue two approaches. They can either be mentioned as a source of knowledge-related queries in the Knowledge Graph, or they can name and present your company in the Knowledge Graph for company-related searches.

Google Knowledge Graph on the right side

How to create a Google Knowledge Graph Panel

Google obtains most of its information from knowledge-based panels from the huge online reference work Wikipedia. Companies that want to appear as a source themselves can access the data labeling via the markup. The search queries made by users are relevant to the Knowledge Graph Panel as opposed to the rich cards and rich snippets schemes such as person and medical entity. Companies and organizations that want to present their company as a Knowledge Graph Panel can use the following criteria as an orientation.

- ✓ The existence of a complete Google My Business profile is mandatory.
- ✓ The website is an authoritarian site that is often quoted or linked by other websites.
- ✓ The company or organization can show predominantly positive evaluations.
- ✓ Active social media profiles are included when creating a Google Knowledge Graph Panel. Facebook, Twitter, LinkedIn and Instagram enjoy a high status and should therefore be integrated during use.
- ✓ A Wikipedia entry for the respective company should also be available.
- ✓ Important company information is available thanks to a markup. This includes company data, executives, the company logo, the brand name and the official social media profiles.

Definition of Featured Snippets

Featured snippets are the last variant of the snippet. They represent short and concise answers that Google presents to its users using an answer box in the search results pages. They are available in three types and consist of a flow form, a list form and a table form.

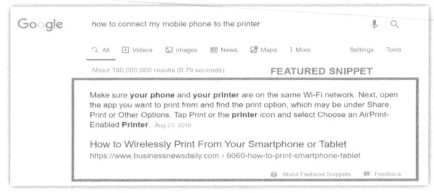

Make sure **your phone** and **your printer** are on the same Wi-Fi network. Next, open the app you want to print from and find the print option, which may be under Share, Print or Other Options. Tap Print or the **printer** icon and select Choose an AirPrint-Enabled **Printer**. Aug 23, 2019

How to Wirelessly Print From Your Smartphone or Tablet
https://www.businessnewsdaily.com › 6060-how-to-print-smartphone-tablet

Featured Snippet in Google Search

How to create featured snippets

Companies that aim to find their organization in such a "response box" must use appropriate keywords. Google does not use the featured snippets for all search queries, because not every single search term is important from a traffic perspective. However, the chance of an ad in the response box only exists for websites that are in the top ten of the search results or, ideally, in the top three. Therefore an intensive examination of the tool called Sistrix, Searchmetrics or Ahrefs is worthwhile in order to see the keywords with which a good ranking can be achieved. Whereby Ahrefs is not free of charge.

Filtering by keyword ranking using featured snippets at Sistrix

Webmasters who have found interesting keywords with a good search volume can then take action to "annex" this featured snippet with appropriate content. The structure used plays a special role here. In this case, however, structured data is not a mandatory prerequisite, but merely a plus point. Webmasters should present their visible texts skilfully with stylistic means.

    ✓   Continuous text form: Webmasters who opt for optimization with a continuous text form answer box must find short informative answers to a keyword that is often contained in the questions. The optimal length of an answer is between 40 and 50 words. Keywords such as "definition" or "by which we mean" have proven themselves in practice. Google thus receives the information that these are helpful explanations that offer users added value

- ✓ List form: When using lists, the ideal length is four to a maximum of five entries consisting of ten terms. However, it is worthwhile to include more points than Google can present. Such an approach increases the likelihood of clicking, as the users usually want to read the other points as well. Signal terms such as instructions, preparation, checklist and guide have proven to be extremely effective keywords. Other terms that encourage you to click on them also belong in the table. They consist of the words "find, make and click here".
- ✓ Table form: Those who select a response box in table form must also display it on their website. The table should consist of three to four rows and two to three columns. After a revision of the website, webmasters should apply for a re-crawling at Google. This is possible via the crawling function called retrieval as by Google, which is located in the Search Console.

Conclusion

It is not a work of art on Google to use structured data to achieve greater attention. Even if the first glance at the topic suggests the opposite. The digital marketers must not be afraid of the markup. These directly influence the content presentation of the web pages in the search results. There are numerous possibilities at this point, which require either no or only minimal IT knowledge. Those who overcome this hurdle are guaranteed to enjoy a much higher click-through rate with a significantly higher number of visitors.

2.8

A GUIDE TO OFF-PAGE OPTIMIZATION

It is not a work of art on Google to use structured data to achieve greater attention. Even if the first glance at the topic suggests the opposite. The digital marketers must not be afraid of the markup. These directly influence the content presentation of the web pages in the search results. There are numerous possibilities at this point, which require either no or only minimal IT knowledge. Those who overcome this hurdle are guaranteed to enjoy a much higher click-through rate with a significantly higher number of visitors.

Definition of Off-Page SEO

The term "Off-Page SEO" stands for all efforts that site administrators make in the background to increase their success in the display of a search engine. A large number of users only connect Off-Page SEO with a link structure. The activity mentioned above involves much more than the creation of links. The distinction between On- and Off-Page SEO is uncomplicated. The former stands for activities within a homepage, whereas Off-Page SEO stands for actions that take place outside the website.

Prepare pages for link building

Links still represent an important component for Google. The search engine can be difficult to determine the value of a website if no links refer to it. It plays a subordinate role how meaningful, extensive or current the page content is. Many side operators are tempted to ignore the preparations for the necessary link building. Those who follow the rules below will make a big contribution to ensuring the success of your website.

Carry out internal organization of the page in advance

Internal page optimizations make a significant difference for overarching positions. Experts also understand this to mean a link between the pages. Keywords take over the linking function. Brian Deans has earned himself a reputation as the "best known SEO expert". He wrote a valuable article entitled "Google's 200 Ranking Factors", mentioning that the amount of internal links to a selected page represents its importance over other subpages of the same website.

The technical term for this procedure is "creating silo pages". They form a symbiosis to the category pages and the supporting pages. SEO experts speak of a link jewel of a backlink that improves search results. That is why smart SEO professionals use links cleverly by organizing their pages in such a way that each individual link leads its respective SEO Juice to further subpages. SEO Juice is also called Link Juice. This stands for a backlink to a page that improves search results. Another basic rule, which stands for Off-Page SEO, is that none of the internal pages should be a loner. Every existing main and subpage is an integral part of the entire website for successful web designers. This in turn scores with seamless navigation. This is a necessary condition both for the users and for the search results. Ideally, there should be a link to pages whose subject areas are related to each other. Readers benefit most from such content.

However, internal sites still suffer from stepmotherly treatment. Even SEO consultants sometimes forget that the internal page structure also determines the SEO value. Silos do not only function as valuable thematic focal points, but also enable the forwarding between the pages. It is not the number of internal links that plays a role, but their quality.

Experienced SEO consultants, however, consider backlinks as the most significant off-page SEO factors. Natural links from major foreign websites with a certain subject size take on the role of an independent vote of confidence, which helps webmasters to consolidate credibility in the search engine. The search spiders, who enjoyed a detailed explanation at the beginning of the book, visit pages and crawl for current content. They then index the new pages that they prepare for users. Websites that have made the leap into the powerful index and appear in search results as soon as users perform meaningful searches, Google uses several factors to decide where to place the page. SEO experts speak of the Google ranking factors that are required for organic searches. The number of factors is a digit that is greater than 200 and increases.

The most important SEO ranking factor, however, is the impact of the links. Once upon a time, the rule was that the more links to a website, the more likely Google was to be ranked as more important. The quality of the links played a subordinate role in the past. Meanwhile the links enjoy a different status. Numerous questions arise when Google finds a link to a website. The first question relates to the origin of the link. This is followed by the question as to why a page operator refers to a selected page. The importance of authority also requires classification. In addition, the topicality of the link plays a decisive role. Invalid and outdated links annoy users. Since the Google Penguin Update, backlinks should also take into account that they are niche relevant. A car dealership that receives a back link from an auto blog is much more successful. The link of a general page, on the other hand, does not deliver the same success.

Therefore, the following link strategies are intended to act as a useful guide for webmasters dedicated to off-page SEO. These are tactics that almost anyone can apply to their website. Furthermore, these procedures increase the number of site visitors and thus contribute to the success of the company. But before web site designers begin to apply the following tactics, they should know the difference between a strategy and a tactic. The first refers to a comprehensive plan, whereas the last is used when the achievement of an objective is pursued. A single link building strategy is perfectly sufficient. However, in order to realize a successful link building for the Off-Page SEO, webmasters should consider the strategy as an engine and the tactic as a tool necessary for a successful running of the engine. The following nine tactics can serve as orientation for achieving a successful link building strategy.

❶ Realizing a wide reach - closing outreach gaps

Link building tactics are the first to focus on a good reach. The focus is on the term "outreach", which stands for finding customers in their niche and making the website content known. However, there is one aspect that webmasters should not neglect and that is that content is not absolutely necessary. The existence of a product, service, brand, personality and company is sufficient. Many website designers link their pages to "ahrefs.com" when they want to implement a link building strategy. This is due to the numerous useful tools that Ahrefs offers its users. Two groups are important when it comes to "Generating a higher reach". Group one consists of customers who mention the main keywords of a product, service or other offer in their articles. The second group consists of webmasters who link to similar topics. The Content Explorer is suitable for finding the first group. This is a tool in which entering a single word or phrase is enough to obtain nearly one billion web pages with matching results. Once the results have been displayed, users can click on "One article per domain". You will then receive a list of individual pages that you can use to increase your reach. All the webmasters have to do is locate the contact information and send an e-mail to potential customers. Potential customers who have linked to similar topics can be selected and contacted using an integrated filter available in the Content Explorer.

❷ Varied guest blogging with an add-on

Guest blogging is one of the oldest link building tactics. It is also characterized by a comprehensible simplicity. A web page designer simply writes a text for another page in his niche. Afterwards the other side publishes the article and the author links to his own homepage. However, the most important question is: How do authors get so-called guest contributions? Fortunately, there are numerous sites on the net that are actively searching for guest bloggers. A Google search operator has proven to be particularly valuable in practice. The searched terms are: "Subject + Title "Write for us". Interested authors will receive pages created to attract guest bloggers in response to this search request. However, the majority of web site creators do so. That is why the time has come for a change. A blog called "Ahrefsblog" can illustrate this as a successful example. The site accepts interesting texts from the guests, although it does not refer to them. In order to find pages that present similar content, it is worth using the Ahref Content Explorer. However, this tool is not free. Users can switch to free tools. The mentioned tools are small search engines. Web page designers can enter any word and receive nearly one billion web pages in response. In addition, the "One article per web page" delimitation helps to delimit the relevant pages. The next step is to filter the unwanted pages with the already integrated filters. Afterwards it is necessary to "export" the relevant pages using a CSV file in order to save the relevant pages. The result is a clearly arranged list containing several hundred pages that are relevant for a potential guest contribution. The next step consists of the action of getting into contact, the publication of the topic and the guest contribution.

❸ The benefits of broken link building

The so-called Broken Link Building is another off-page tactic and consists of three steps. The first step is to find a broken link of a website. Step two requires the creation of an internet presence that resembles the source with the broken link or offers this added value. In the last step, webmasters ask anyone who refers to the dead link to refer to the newly created one. One question that emerges from this is: "How can webmasters find significant methods to drive the construction of broken links? There are many ways to achieve this result. The fastest way is to search for broken links on the websites of competitors. Reports of the "Best by Links" in the Site Explorer of the respective tool provide an enormous remedy. These reports usually indicate the number of referring domains that contain broken links. Webmasters will find a lot of relevant pages that they can use for their own purposes.

④ Unrelated mentions

From time to time, persons, products, offers or services may be mentioned by other website operators without being directly linked by them. In practice, this happens more often than expected. The challenge is to identify the unrelated but relevant mentions. The already mentioned Content Explorer from Ahrefs is suitable as a tool to find unmentioned links. Users should keep in mind, however, that the clever Explorer searches nearly one billion web pages for the terms entered. This can be beneficial in two ways. On the one hand, website operators can use this method to find pages that deal with a particular topic. On the other hand, they can check in this way how often their trademark is mentioned throughout the Internet. However, an automatic display of relevant pages does not provide an answer to the question whether the mentions are also linked to the target website. To clarify this, webmasters export all web pages and check whether each one refers to the "company name.com". Those who don't know the following trick spend a lot of time checking the references. Experienced administrators select the filter named "One article per domain" in the Content Explorer. Thanks to this selection, the filter limits the number of search results many times over. It displays only one web page from each page. Web page designers then use the "Mark unlinked domains" feature to locate any Web pages that have not been linked to the target Web page. The selected web pages are then exported using the "Export" command. The checkbox "Select only unlinked domains" should be activated. The result is a manageable table of homepages with unlinked mentions that users can study at their leisure.

⑤ Link Complaint

Successful link building is more complicated than expected. There are no two ways to accomplish this task. In addition, many webmasters do not know that they often lose their backlinks. Of course, this process can be slowed down by constantly creating new links. But restoring the lost links makes much more sense than creating new links. The crucial question at this point, however, is why links are lost. There are two reasons for this phenomenon. First, the link has been removed from the link page. Second, the entire linking page has been disabled. However, these are not the only two reasons why links disappear. If the first reason is true, it is most likely due to the content update of the author's website. As a rule, they remove the links, as they represent an unusable by-product in their eyes. Users who discover that the link has been removed due to a content revision can contact the website operator and suggest a new link. However, there are many other reasons why links are lost. Therefore, website operators should take a close look at this topic and understand why their link is not found on the respective page. But what happens to links that no longer exist because the link page has been deleted? As a rule, the cause of this loss lies in a complete deletion of the page. If this is the case, users cannot do much about it. Sometimes, however, pages are accidentally deleted. Webmasters who take this view with their lost link should contact the website operator and inform him of this information immediately. Most of the time, they rebuild the page and the link when they are notified of the problem. This reference is valuable in two ways, as it also provides the foundation for a good relationship from which further connections can emerge.

⑥ Paid promotions for "linkable assets"
Linkable assets are among the components that are worth a link. These include various tools, calculators, detailed, informative and instructive blog posts, learning programs and infographics. However, there is another method to inform the target group about the content. This requires a small financial investment. Facebook ads, Google AdWords and Pinterest ads can only be used against payment. As a rule, between 40 and 90 euros are sufficient for this. Contents that correspond to a selected target group benefit from a link. This can be done via the main website, a comment on another blog, or a discussion forum. Paid promotions are an extremely complicated process from a technical point of view. This ignores algorithms that explore search queries and display matching search results based on them. Therefore, advertisers appear before the actual ranking winners in the results. Of course this advertisement is marked. If users don't have an ad blocker installed in their browser, Google presents the advertisers' ads to them first. This example shows that webmasters can also enjoy the top position for a fee.

⑦ Copying links from inferior pages
In this step, web page designers look for other pages whose links are not good. Thereupon they develop better content and ask for exchange of the linking, through their own website. This approach enables a niche relevant backlink strategy.

8 Reuse and syndicate content

However, the link building tactics presented here do not focus exclusively on a large reach. Webmasters can also create links by submitting only educational content to appropriate locations. Infographics directories, websites that present videos and share them belong to the said contents. The condition for a successful transmission of the contents is the use of a suitable format. At this point the Repurposing of the interesting content is used. Those who have put a lot of work into a presentable interactive graphic often feel the desire to share it with other users on the go. To do this, however, they must convert the created content into a universal info graphic or video format. After formatting, webmasters can send the content to so-called infographics or video sharing sites. Webmasters can also link their created content to other third-party websites. Thus interesting blog contributions profit in several respects, since they are called up by other web pages and are led including left to the source. There are websites that either publish the entire content as a document, but others present only one section and place a link that leads to the complete post of the respective page.

9 Link building using community sites

The majority of webmasters make the mistake of concentrating only on links of the highest quality. In principle they are on the right side with this approach. Back link profiles, which however should appear lively and loose, are not only composed of editorial links. Clever website designers create a successful mix of backlinks by using forums, message boards, Reddit Quora or other types of text. Diversification makes a small but subtle difference. Therefore, writing blog comments worth reading is a good way to create additional links. Blog comments are usually so-called "follow up links". Interesting comments, however, benefit from a larger audience. This approach can increase the number of links because a certain percentage of the readers who present the content refer to the link. The challenge, however, is to find good blog posts that deserve a comment. Webmasters switch to the Content Explorer and enter a relevant sentence or search term. The next step is the filtration of the pages that have usable data traffic. Then a check of the results and whether the respective pages allow blog comments takes place. If comment features are allowed, webmasters should write an insightful comment that makes readers think and leads to the target web page. In addition, leaving behind successful blog comments attracts the blogger's attention and can have a beneficial effect on the relationship. He can also mention the person who has written good comments in other blog articles and link to the target page. The Quora page can also help with link building. **Is a link purchase possible?** Interested webmasters can purchase links at a monetary price. Link building is not an unlearnable science. All the tactics presented in this book can be applied unconditionally to all websites. Some tactics are better suited for some online appearances, others less so. The challenge for webmasters is to find the best tactics for their website.

root domain   test.de

19,293 of 20,000 queries available until 06/30

Domain Authority [i]	Linking Domains [i]	Inbound Links [i]	Ranking Keywords [i]
88	35.5k	5.3m	701
	Discovered in the last 60 days 928		
	Lost in last 60 days 1.4k		

Section of a Domain Authority (DA) from the SEO tool "MOZ"

Experts strongly advise against relying solely on Domain Authority metrics. Focusing on a single measure such as the Domain Authority (DA) provides unreliable and inaccurate results. Only a holistic view can provide reliable values with regard to the evaluation of traffic, engagement and relevance. Metrics, which originate from the different tools of search engine optimization, receive harsh criticism. It doesn't matter whether it is Ahrefs, Moz, MajesticSEO or another tool. Since their introduction, they have been a hotly debated topic. The domain authority from the well-known Moz tool was also criticized. Moz announced a comprehensive upgrade of DA-Metric and assured that it was more trustworthy. But the difficulty lies in the way the DA is used. In the following, some basic questions that prevent the majority of companies from using DA-Metric are explained.

The biggest problem of the DA is a possible misuse of metrics. SEO beginners often make the mistake of focusing on just one metric. They concentrate only on getting links to a certain metric. However, they should focus on increasing the number of DAs. Meanwhile a complete SEO industry exists, which is specialized in the sale of DA-Links. The challenge, however, is to determine the strength of a page or link by focusing on a single metric like the DA. This is simply inaccurate and unreliable in equal measure.

❶ Third party metrics

Currently, Moz uses about 40 factors to determine the DA scores. These also include the linking of the root domains as well as the multitude of the entire links. The problem is that the underlying data is not complex enough to accurately determine the ability of a domain to rank and the true link strength originating from a domain. Google has been on the Internet since 1993. There is also a reason why the company has become the market leader in the field of search technology. Experts suspect that Google's algorithms use at least 200 factors to evaluate a page ranking. Google's constant, rapid and complex development proves that it cannot match such a simple metric system as the DA.

❷ Make appropriate predictions

According to experts, both an increase and a decrease in DA is not related to a change in ranking. It is merely a prediction of hypothetical developments.

❸ PageRank

PageRank was once Google's secret metric, but it became public in 2000. Besides, she lost her status. This was because people did not want to commit themselves to a single metric. Furthermore, the PageRank alone does not determine the determined position of a web page. In fact, this was a combination of several factors and the PageRank score. Concentrating on a single metric served more as a distraction. For years, many Google experts have asserted that they have no internal counterpart to the so-called website authority. The fact that a single valuation is not sufficient for the valuation is sufficient evidence of the need for several factors.

❹ Manipulations are possible

Rankings on Google can still be falsified to a certain degree. This shows how easily DA values can be manipulated. Also, counterfeiting a DA score is not a big problem.

❺ Relevance is a decisive factor

Webmasters who rely only on a measure like DA forget to include the things that are necessary when creating links. Every now and then you forget to ask yourself whether the link is relevant in terms of content. They also do not ask themselves whether the content of the displayed page offers visitors a real added value. To answer these questions, the webmasters do not need a metric system. Therefore, website designers should not focus so much on the DA metrics, even though a large number of link builders rely on the DA as a basis and use it to create links with a certain score. If used properly, DA metrics can even provide valuable information about why some websites cannot improve their rank. For that reason it is worthwhile to use DA metrics sparingly.

Nevertheless, the webmasters should disregard the metrics that actually count. Traffic, relevance and commitment provide added value. Those who focus on these three metrics can benefit in many ways.

Consider the competition's off-page strategy

In order to be able to rank over the competitors who also operate SEO, webmasters should analyze their strategy. Where does the competition get their backlinks from? Back link tools from MOZ or Ahrefs provide a decisive hint to this question. With these the backlinks can eliminate the competitors. This requires a click on the competitor's back-link sources. Then the regional pages are linked to the competitors (this tactic is worthwhile with regard to the Local SEO), online magazines and online newspaper portals. However, site operators must ask themselves whether these are merely purchased guest contributions. The question of whether the backlinks are relevant to the topic should also be clarified. In addition, the answer to the question of whether the pages have high metrics is also helpful. An analysis of whether competitors are working with content marketing is essential. Web designers should ask themselves all these questions if they have found a suitable competitor who also operates a successful SEO. If the analyzed competitors have good back-link sources, webmasters can use them. This is the case when a regional newspaper links to a competitor. Why shouldn't the newspaper link to the target page? Webmasters should offer added value to the online newspaper. Still, web designers should be strictly careful to implement a better SEO strategy. For this reason, they should use a second high-quality back link from another regional online newspaper and also add topic-relevant backlinks from their niche. In addition, they should be of high quality.

 Tip:

Do not forget your free SEO-Analysis for further information.
Get it now **www.seomarkt.de/premium**
Password: **SEO2019DE89**

The Underestimated Importance of Local SEO

3.0

DEFINITION

Local SEO is becoming more and more important for companies and other organizations because the number of competitors is constantly increasing. The proportion of users who use mobile devices to make their search queries is also constantly on the rise. Similarly, the number of searches that are characterized by a local reference is growing. Local SEO aims to make companies and their online presence as well-known as possible in local search results. But before this happens, webmasters are forced to follow a certain number of

Google MyBusiness Presentation

special conditions of the ranking. This chapter goes into the necessary factors in detail. For companies with a local presence, it is important to have a strong presence in Google's local search results. Local search queries are increasing, thanks to the high number of users of mobile devices. Mobile devices are proof of this trend. Only a small number of users make local search queries via the desktop. Most users make their requests when they are on the move. Classic examples of this are: "Where's the nearest gas station?" "Where is an emergency pharmacy?" "What time can I get groceries in my neighborhood?" As a result of this development, almost 25 percent of all search results now contain a so-called "local pack". This is a box, which presents selected and locally significant search results extra prominently. Unfortunately the space of a Local Pack is small. Usually no more than five companies, medical practices, service providers or other organizations make it into this box. Local search results also appear in other places on Google. These include the Local Panel, Google Maps and organic search results.

The Local Panel appears on the right side of the SERP, which is an abbreviation for Search Engine Result Page. SERPs illustrate the results of search queries. Local panels, on the other hand, display information about the organization.

This includes the address, telephone number, customer ratings and a map showing the location. In order to appear at these points of view, those responsible must know and apply the necessary ranking factors, which are described in detail in the following section. Local panels also provide information for local companies, organizations and other institutions via tab navigation. These enable users to quickly access the information they need. Those who are looking for a restaurant near them can click directly on the menu using the "menu".

3.2

IMPORTANT RANKING FACTORS OF THE LOCAL SEO

Analogous to the organic search, important factors also have a decisive influence on the ranking of local search queries. The US service provider Moz carried out a study on this subject in 2017. The most important factor of Local SEO is called Google My Business. In second place are the Backlinks. Third and fourth place went to ON Page Op-

Google MyBusiness Display

timization and Citations. This is followed by reviews, user behavior, personalization and social factors. The study also shows how closely the ranking factors correspond to those of the organic search. The study also confirms the importance of ON page optimization and backlinks. However, the so-called citations, ratings and Google My Business are of particular importance.

① Google My Business - a cornerstone for success in local search engine optimization - Google My Business is a Google feature that presents local search results to users. The individuals are looking for companies, service providers or restaurants that are in the immediate vicinity of their current location. Local search results appear in different places on Google Maps and Google Search. Those who enter the search term "Greek restaurant" usually receive local search results. The results page then presents suitable restaurants that are close to the seekers. Companies that don't show up on the local search results page should review their data entry and then follow the steps below on Google My Business. This increases the visibility for existing and potential customers many times over.

② Enter data completely
Local search results prefer the most meaningful results for the given search query. Companies that have provided both complete and exact information definitely score points. This is because they can be better assigned to requests than organizations that leave important fields blank. First, however, a registration takes place before the data input takes place. Companies that have registered with Google My Business can then not only list their location, the relevant industry, a current telephone number, but also the opening hours and upload pictures. Complete data entry significantly improves the company's ranking chances in local search results.

③ Carry out location confirmation
A verification of the My Business entry is indispensable. Therefore, Google, in most cases, sends a postcard to the address left behind to ensure the existence of the specified location. With this procedure Google wants to counteract the manipulation as well as the indication of incorrect addresses. For this reason, companies urgently need to confirm their locations. The verification of the geographical location where the organization is located is also necessary so that users who use the two Google services, such as Google Maps or Google Search, actually find the companies.

4 Regularly check that opening hours are up to date

Data maintenance for opening hours is particularly important, as users who locate a company via Local SEO want to know whether it is worth going to the organization specified. For this reason, those responsible for a company must enter the opening hours. They should also inform their customers of the special opening hours on Sundays and public holidays.

5 Edit and respond to reviews

Responsible companies are aware of the importance of customer contact for the continued existence of an economically oriented organization. Therefore, account managers interact with their customers by taking a clear stance on their reviews. Answering customer evaluations signals the company's appreciation of its customers. In addition, select and positive customer ratings improve a company's visibility in the local search. Moreover, affirmative reviews increase the probability of further customer inflows. Therefore, a link to a selected website, on which visitors and customers can leave reviews, is a necessary condition that contributes to the success of the company.

6 Bring the entry to life with photos

Experienced entrepreneurs know how to give their entry a personal touch. They decorate their notes with photos. These help the customers with the optical internalization of the company. A corporate brand is ultimately an image that is permanently anchored in the perception of customers. For this reason, decorating the entry with the company building and logo pays off in two ways. In addition, appealing images signal to customers that they have found exactly what they were looking for.

7 Relevance stands for the match between the result and the search.

The expression "Relevance" symbolizes the match of the local entry with the search query of the user. A detailed and complete provision of information increases the probability of being classified as a relevant company in search queries.

8 **The distance is sometimes decisive for the visit of the company.** The distance stands for the distance between the location of the search query and the respective location to the company. However, if the request does not have a current location, the distance is calculated using the data known about the user and his usual whereabouts. Awareness - a decisive factor in search queries Companies with a high level of awareness are more likely to appear on the search results page than those that are not known to users. Famous brands, hotels, restaurant chains take the lead in the search re-sults. The awareness arises partly in the Internet. Their origin lies in the numerous links, articles and directories. The Google ratings of the visitors also determine the ranking status of the local search results. The greater the number of reviews, the better the rated company scores in the ranking. Furthermore, the position of the company in the search results is decisive. In addition, the so-called Best Practices, which have already been explained, also apply to the ON-Page-SEO with regard to the best possible design of the lo-cal search results. Determination of the ranking of the local search results.

Distance, relevance and **awareness** are therefore the three critical factors that determine the ranking of Google search results. A combination of these three factors provides users with relevant hits that are closest to their search query.

3.3

BACKLINKS - AN INDISPENSABLE PART OF LOCAL SEO

Google also counts on specified backlinks in the local search. The details play an important role here. The goal is to create numerous select and up-to-date backlinks from different domains, which also show a local context or industry reference. For this reason, links from other organizations such as suppliers and customers in the area who are active in a similar or even the same indus-try are optimal. backlinks also contain anchor texts. These also require careful maintenance, as they send Google another signal of relevance. The basic rules explained for ON-Page Optimization apply to both organic and local searches.

However, experts divide the number of relevant factors into several areas. Technical search engine optimization is the top priority, as it concerns loading time, encrypted transmission via https and mobile friendliness. With regard to the design, the webmasters must also not allow themselves any slip-ups. The texts convince with their high quality and are provided with professional pictures. Furthermore, the page structure follows a logical division and is divided into meaningful categories. Users prefer perfect operability, clarity and legibility. The last aspect relates in particular to people with visual impairment. They are pleased about sides, whose contents also they can understand, despite handicap. Webmasters who take these criteria into account when calculating local SEO will benefit from a better ranking result. NAP is an abbreviation for "Name, Address and Phone". These data represent an important special feature in Local SEO. It is advantageous to indicate these on each page and to design them uniformly.

Local Citations - a useful marketing tool for local organizations

Those who are urgently concerned with search engine optimization for locally active organizations will eventually come across the term "local citations". Territorial online marketing is indispensable for both small and medium-sized enterprises (SMEs). Every single click increases the probability of winning another customer. However, the term Local Citations requires a detailed definition and explanation of how Local SEO works. In the following a detailed explanation of the technical term is given.

3.4

DEFINITION OF LOCAL CITATIONS

Local Citations stands for the naming of an organization including local data such as name, address and telephone number on the Internet. Citations appear on all types of websites. Blogs, press sites, forums or sites of associations present local citations. Nevertheless, they are preferably to be found on the pages of the digital yellow pages. These include the website GelbeSeiten.de, meineStadt.de, Golocal.Google and Yelp. Google obtains part of its information from the industry portals mentioned. In the meantime, numerous different directories exist. They can be cross-industry or cross-city. In addition, industry-specific and locally oriented portals are also present. However, companies must consider whether their organization is suitable for an entry on a particular website.

3.5

THE CONNECTION BETWEEN THE LOCAL CITATIONS AND THE LOCAL SEARCH

Google is the most frequently used search engine in Germany and therefore enjoys a special status. That is why Google's goal is to show searchers only the best results when searching for a local service provider or business. To achieve this goal of the best possible results, Google has introduced its own business directory with local maps such as Google Maps. In addition, the most popular search engine in Germany pulls the registered information from the directories and portals in order to determine relevant data of a company. Google checks the accuracy of the data and also determines the company's location using the entries. The more often a company with the same name, address and telephone number appears in these directories, the less likely Google is to doubt the existence of the business or the accuracy of the data. A frequent appearance of a company stands for its activity and authenticity. In addition, a regular appearance on the search query contributes to a better place in the ranking.

Therefore, companies should observe the following rules in order to increase or maintain their success in ranking.

- ✓ Company names should always be displayed identically. If there is a company addition like GmbH, OHG or GbR, then the responsible persons must indicate this with each entry.
- ✓ The contact numbers given must not differ from each other. This also includes strict observance of the spaces.
- ✓ Obsolete addresses or invalid opening hours are also out of place.

Online yellow pages thus have a direct influence on Google's ranking. The following example illustrates the need for correct data entry.

There is a long list of classified directories on the Internet. In addition, not every organization can access all portals. Companies should not pursue the goal of leaving a citation in all directories. It depends rather on a selective and correct selection of one or more suitable portals. In marketing, companies that pursue a clear strategy such as price leadership or quality strategy achieve significant advantages over their competitors. The same applies to the use of Local Citations. The choice of strategy is a basic building block for success. In the first step, those responsible should check which data they are listed with on the Internet. "Omnea" has proven itself in practice as a helpful site for checking the information already available. This page provides a free instant check that shows users which business directories their organization is listed in.

Local Citations are important for small, medium and large companies. This is particularly true when the respective organizations are represented at several locations. Companies that want to be found by a potential clientele have to score with a good online presence. Google prefers a location with multiple local citations to those with a small number of citations. A link to the company's website is not necessary, as the organization's name, address and telephone number are sufficient. However, experts recommend that companies pay much more attention to quality than quantity when using citations. Furthermore, experts continue to believe that industry relevance plays a crucial role in relation to citations. These can occur in different ways in the network. There are online citations without a link. These are organizations that are listed in a portal, but do not contain a back link as a hint. Whereas the Citations with Back Link also contain a Back Link to the company website. Offline citations mention companies in offline media such as daily newspapers or other print media. This allows residents to enter their name in Google and open their Google MyBusiness listing. Thus local visitors come on the MyBusiness entry. Google also has the position of the companies at its disposal thanks to GPS. For this reason, offline citations have a passively positive effect on the ranking. All three versions can have an effect on the local ranking. Their influence, however, depends on the medium on which they are present. Citations with opening hours and a complete data entry are still the most helpful. Companies can select industry-specific directories or niche sites as a source for the right directory selection. These should be adapted to the topic which corresponds to the offers and services of the respective organization. Offline campaigns such as mentions in the Yellow Pages and small ads in a daily newspaper can also have a positive effect on the local ranking. In this way they assure the search engines that they really exist in the place mentioned.

Choosing the right business directory with regard to Local Citations

Company entries have a positive effect on the online presence of a company. Industry portals serve the same purpose as the former printed Yellow Pages. Consumers will find in the numerous entries, doctors, painters or lawyers who are in their immediate vicinity. However, the design of the classified directories on the Internet differs considerably. There are portals that are locally oriented, directories that have been defined for specific industries, and platforms that link the two components together in a meaningful way. Companies that want to find out which directory suits them best can enter different keyword combinations into Google. An example of this would be "Barber + New York", "Gym + New York", "Dinner + New York". After a thorough review of the first pages that deliver good search results, companies get a good overview of directories that often appear and score with a good positioning.

Webmasters who look at the search results of the first few pages get an overview of which portals appear most frequently and are particularly well positioned.

1. Supra-regional and cross-industry platforms are extremely interesting for most companies because they list all industries in all cities. They then sort them carefully. These include "yellowpages.com" or "here.com".
2. There are also regional and cross-sector directories. There are regions in which an above-average number of these platforms are present, while others have only a small number of portals. The company is therefore dependent on the region in which it is located.
3. In addition, there are platforms that only provide information on selected industries. However, they have not defined themselves as a region, but refer to the entire national territory. A classic example of such a portal is the "dentistsrecommend.com".
4. Regional and sector-specific portals are rather an exception. They are extremely rare in comparison to the three preceding portals.

In order to be successful with local citations, companies must search for one or more suitable directories. The majority of platforms allow users to make basic entries free of charge. However, the companies have to pay for the extended premium entries. The use of the latter is only worthwhile, however, if the business directory is a highly frequented one. Moreover, premium entries do not benefit from a better ranking factor. It is sufficient to provide the company name, address and contact details. In addition, the choice of the appropriate directory depends on the location of the company and the sector in question. The following list shows the most relevant industry portals that are enjoying great popularity among companies.

r.	Site	Domain Authority (DA)	Niche
	maps.apple.com	100	General
	facebook.com	94	General
	yelp.com	94	General
	bing.com	94	General
	foursquare.com	92	General
	local.yahoo.com	92	General
	mapquest.com	90	General
	here.com	88	General
	yellowpages.com	87	General
0	tomtom.com	82	General

3.6

THE ROLE OF REVIEWS AND RATINGS IN LOCAL SEO

Reviews and ratings play an important role in Local SEO. Marketing reports on the behaviour of customers and divides this into experience, search and trust characteristics.

Individuals can only evaluate the characteristics of experience and trust once they have made use of a specific service or an offer from a company. Therefore, reviews are important for potential customers, as they decide whether they will use the services offered by a company. Experience reports are a reliable indicator of the quality of a company's services and products. Not only the reviews that appear on Google are important, but also those that appear on portals such as Trust Pilot or Yelp. Buyers and users can express their individual opinions on numerous websites. Amazon, Facebook Review and Rating, TripAdvisor or Yahoo! Local Listings are among the sites that provide credible reviews.

The company's own website also provides valuable information for customer evaluations. However, these require the use of structured data. Only then is Google able to evaluate these. These will be explained later. Ratings act as recommendations for a website, analogous to backlinks. In recent times there have been a lot of wrong reviews on the Internet. Such deceptions, however, violate Google's policies. Meanwhile, Google can recognize the fake ratings and assign them to a penalty, which in turn results in the exclusion of the respective organization from the local ranking. In order to benefit from favorable valuations, companies can fall back on numerous legitimate methods. This includes among other things the request for a product evaluation after the purchase. Online shops send their customers e-mails asking them to express their satisfaction with their last purchase. Many companies also often contact their satisfied customers and ask them to help with a review. Large mail order companies motivate their customers to leave feedback on their homepage by sending them a voucher with a monetary value after a certain number of evaluations.

Positive evaluations are important for Local SEO, as potential customers rely on them as much as possible and decide to use the company's service or product depending on the experience reports.

3.7

STRUCTURE DATA AND ITS ROLE IN LOCAL SEO

Structured data symbolize the highlighting of selected elements on a homepage. These have already been explained in detail in chapter XY (placeholders for correct numbering). In addition, different HTML tags and attributes help with identification. Data such as opening hours, company name, address, telephone number, product descriptions, prices and reviews are also important identification attributes. The mentioned data do not represent a ranking factor in the search engines, but can increase the probability of several clicks. Webmasters who do not want to change their HTML code to highlight the structured data can use the Google Data Highlighter. This is a tool that can be found in the Google Search Console. A practical graphical interface helps to mark individual elements on the website. After successful integration of the structured data, the result is checked using the Structured Data Testing Tool.

THE LOCATION OF THE USER AND THE DISTANCE TO THE ENTERPRISE ARE DECISIVE

The above ranking factors are only relevant for Local SEO if the distance between the user's location and the company being searched for is not too great. Organizations whose addresses are located outside cities perform worse in search results. They rarely appear on Local Packs for requests for "Keyword" or "City". Google's Opossum update helps disadvantaged companies better integrate with search queries. Nevertheless, the local companies win in the search results. For this reason, experts recommend the use of a physical address within a nearby location for which the companies want to appear in the local results.

Offline actions are not to be neglected here

Google aims to provide users with results that add real value to their experience. The click rate serves as a control factor for this situation. Results that appear high up in the search but are still ignored by users probably do not match their expectations. Thus, other search results must be placed in the upper ranks. However, Google can use other methods to perform a quality measurement in local search optimization. Suppose a user receives a local search result and clicks on it. This could be the nearest health food store. If the user then visits the store and stays there for a while, Google receives the information that the search results provided have met the user's expectations. The customer can then rate the shop on Google My Business. The smartphone sends the location signal to Google. That is why Google knows if the user was actually in the store. If the customer visits the store again after a certain period of time, Google rates the further purchase as positive. This means that the user was satisfied and the store meets customer requirements. For this reason, the store can get a better place in the ranking. This example is a wonderful illustration of how close the boundaries between the online and offline worlds are in the local search. For this reason, not only the quality of the website and the My Business entry determine the place in the ranking, but also the nature of the products and services offered. However, in order to be found by users, companies must register in the online business directories. In the following there is an explanation for a successful implementation.

THE SUCCESSFUL CREATION AND OPTIMIZATION OF LOCAL LANDING PAGES

A local landing page aims to reach the right customers. There are websites that record more than 100,000 visitors per month, but still achieve a low turnover. In contrast, other sites enjoy a significantly higher profit, although only 20,000 potential product buyers visit the respective site. The reason for this paradoxical example lies in the correct recognition and finding of the target group. This is particularly evident from the practical location activity map. The so-called peer group is relevant for page optimization, as it contains relevant information such as customer wishes. The term peer group stands for a group of people who share common interests, origin, age and similar social status. The group represents an orientation for the individual. The knowledge of the location of the website visitors is worthwhile in every respect. Because that raises two questions. The first is:

Which locations should the potential customers come from? And secondly: What are the names of the locations from which the current local customers come? After answering these questions, webmasters can set themselves a clear goal that enables the fulfillment of customer needs. Companies with only one location need only one address and a local telephone number. Customers also receive information as to whether they can visit the organization directly. The possibility of direct contact strengthens customer confidence in the respective company. In order to find out the names of the locations from which the customers come, a login to the previously created Google Analytics account is sufficient. Then a path consisting of five steps leads to the goal. First the search for the Google Analytics Dashboard follows, in the next step the targeting of the target group, then the selection of their interests, the point Geo and after this selection the webmasters receive the information location. This information will help to design the future campaigns and the text on the landing page. However, companies with multiple sites should take this into account when writing their texts and structuring their websites. Therefore in this case it is preferable to focus on the usual SEO. The local search engine optimization is rather disadvantageous there. By practicing the usual search engine optimization, the probability of being visited by a much larger target group increases. However, companies that are limited to a single location can use the local search engine optimization procedures already explained in detail.

Localized metadata increases relevance

The metadata section of the landing page does not differ from the conventional page optimization and consists of title tags, meta descriptions and keywords. Careful maintenance of the three factors mentioned increases the success factor of the website. The metadata is as important as the title tag for OnPage optimization as it is for OnPage optimization.

Optimization of the local landing page for mobile users

The number of local users making searches using mobile devices is growing steadily. Forecasts speak of an upward trend. In the near future, significantly more than 50 percent of the more than 100 billion monthly search queries will be made from mobile devices. For this reason, the telephone number, address or a valid e-mail address is of great importance for local search queries. This is due to the connection between the local search and the condition to find a company which is located in the immediate vicinity of the user site. According to experts, the use of mobile devices is most intensive in the halfway stage of a purchasing process. Therefore, webmasters are forced to reward specific users with a direct approach when they create their local landing pages as well as doorway pages for their local peer group. The immediate proximity to the location is an important factor in optimizing the landing pages for mobile devices. Users usually assume short footpaths and driveways. Another important aspect is the inclusion of the loading times of the websites. In addition, landing pages require special content. Webmasters have to write targeted texts for a group of people to whom they make an offer. The following instructions will help you to create a successful landing page for mobile devices.

1 **Headline design**

The headings on landing pages for mobile devices are extremely short. Ideally, they should consist of a maximum of four words. Every single term that the user does not need can be deleted. A headline bearing the title "Discover our wide range of reduced household appliances" is definitely too long. Whereas the short headline with the words "household appliances - 50 percent discount" is more suitable for a mobile landing page.

❷ Successful presentation of the mobile landing page

Experienced web administrators ensure that all the information users need is presented in a compact form on the mobile landing page version. They put themselves in the position of their website visitors. They always keep in mind how limited the user's time is. Therefore, long descriptions of a product or service offered are out of place. A landing page is also not completely filled with images or text. Instead, all important links and product descriptions are summarized on one page. When designing these specific pages, the saying goes: "Less is more."

❸ Clearly defined calls-to-action

In the case of mobile landing pages, the calls-to-action buttons are characterized by their directness and unambiguous expressiveness. On a mobile landing page, they also represent part of the first element that the user sees.

❹ Telephone number enabling a direct call

Webmasters who want to be called by their potential customers integrate a phone icon or leave a phone number that allows a direct call when clicked. Those who want to be visited by their customers add a link to Google Maps. In this way, users rely on the GPS function of their smartphone to find their way to the corporate location.

❺ Every second counts

With regard to the design of the mobile landing pages, time is a decisive factor. The longer the website visitors have to wait for the homepage to load, the higher the probability that they will leave the site and search for the necessary information from a competitor. That is why every single second counts. Flash technologies or annoying plug-ins take too much time to fully display a page. Therefore, images should be displayed in JPG format. In contrast, PNG images slow down fast page display. HTML5 and JQuery are among the tools that have proven themselves in practice. They have the power to significantly improve loading times. In addition, the number of http requests should be kept low. Instead, CSS images are the better alternative, as they shorten the loading time many times over. Although the ideal size of a mobile landing page depends on the content displayed, the goal should be not to exceed the 20 kilobyte limit. Webmasters should always keep in mind that not all users use the same Internet connection. Some rely on Wi-Fi, others have 4G LTE access and another group uses 3G connections. Of course, it is possible to use an AMP page for this purpose, which has already been extensively presented.

 Test the mobile landing page first

It is worth testing the mobile landing page yourself before it becomes accessible to users. Ideal pages contain little text and clear calls-to-action. The page content should be displayed from the customer's point of view.

> 💡 Tip:
>
> Do not forget your free SEO-Analysis for further information.
> Get it now **www.seomarkt.de/premium**
> Password: **SEO2019DE89**

Voice Search - optimization of websitecontent for voice searches

4.0

D igital language assistants are seeing an increasing number of followers every day. The Google Assistant in particular enjoys great popularity. Both providers of products and companies that sell services
have discovered the benefits of clever language tools. However, this
raises the crucial question: "How does the website content get into the answer
list of the respective language assistants? The following advice is intended as a
guide for webmasters to optimize their content for Voice Search.

According to surveys, more than 50 percent of Internet users have used a digital language assistant as a source of information. A current study commis-
sioned by the Federal Association of the Digital Economy has provided this
finding. The four best-known language assistants used by German Internet
users are Google Assistant, Cortana, Siri and Amazons Alexa. According to the
survey, the majority of users are male and belong to a younger age group. For
this reason, they also take a critical view of the language assistants. In particular, they criticize the possible misuse of data and the monitoring possibilities.
Virtual search assistants score with their speed. These can provide quick information and act as navigation. Comscore is a well-known market research
company that has prepared a forecast for the year 2020. Market researchers
expect that by then every second request will take place with the help of a
voice command. A continuously increasing number of users also implies a better ability of language assistants to use the speech.

PRESENTATION OF THE DIFFERENCES BETWEEN A TRADITIONAL SEARCH AND VOICE SEARCH

Language search queries do not necessarily have to differ from the written search. In contrast to the text-based search, the linguistic search mainly owes its existence to the smartphone. In addition, the latter often has a local reference. Language-based search queries are characterized by specific complexity and dialogues. Users usually pronounce entire sentences or questions in verbal search queries. The main difference between verbal and text-based queries is the formulation of whole sentences. The local reference is another aspect that goes back to the language-based search queries.

Reasons for the rapid development of Voice SEO

One of the main reasons for the uninterrupted progress of Voice SEO is the convenience of the users, who have neither the desire nor the time for long typing. They prefer quick and short answers. Voices are definitely faster than lyrics.

Classification of Voice SEO from the point of view of Google

In connection with the Voice SEO, Google classifies the intentions of users into four categories. **The first** search, which is also the beginning of Voice SEO, is the information search. It is also called the "I Want It Knowing Moment." The number of users looking up information online is now 65 percent. *The value of smartphone users who use their mobile device to search for information they have seen in an advertisement is 66 percent.*

Category number two: "I-Want-To-To-Find-The-Product Or-The-Service-Moment". The search for objects classified by the three terms "near me" has experienced a double increase compared to last year. Today, 82 percent of smartphone users are looking for local businesses by relying on Voice SEO information.

The name of the **third category** is "I-Want-To-do-The-Moment." 91 percent of smartphone users search their mobile phones for ideas while doing a task at the same time. The Voice SEO thus enables multi-tasking.

Category number four means "I want to buy moment". 82 percent of users consult their mobile phones by using the Voice SEO function before deciding on a product in a store.

CONTENT SUITABLE FOR VOICE SEO

Voice Search Engine Optimization is suitable for facts, information and local content. In order to answer such search queries, Google uses web or map results. Furthermore, Google extracts the desired answers from the featured snippets. Webmasters therefore focus on optimizing page content that provides facts, information and local content. The following instructions can serve as a small guide for Voice SEO.

❶ Optimize page content for mobile devices

As a rule, users resort to the verbal search when they are on the move. For this reason, the Mobile First Indexing already explained in this book will gain even more importance. Webmasters must therefore adapt their pages to the requirements of mobile devices. There is a mobile-friendly test from Google. This gives the web designers valuable feedback on whether their site is mobile optimized or not. However, an appealing design is not the only factor webmasters need to consider. Ideally, charging times should not exceed three seconds. The already mentioned Google tool called Pagespeed Insights performs a reliable loading time test. "Thumb-friendliness" is an important building block for a user-friendly mobile website version. The majority of users operate their smartphone either with their index finger or with their thumb. Therefore, the buttons must be large enough so that website visitors can click on them effortlessly without missing them. In addition, the complete page content must be clearly displayed. This applies especially to the texts "above the fold". Users see them first, without scrolling down the page.

❷   Use structured data

Google aims to understand websites as well as possible in order to find out which character of the verbal search queries they most closely match. Website designers can help Google with this task by presenting the content of their site in the best possible way. According to experts, it is worth using structured data such as the Schem.org awards. They enable a useful enrichment of the content with additional information and ideally show search engines which websites are most likely to answer certain search queries.

❸   Include featured snippets in page optimization

Verbal language assistants provide answers to uncomplicated search queries by accessing content from a so-called knowledge graph. For other questions, Google often relies on featured snippets. These are stressed search results. They contain a concise answer from a suitable website. Furthermore, they consist of different formats such as texts, tables, lists or videos. These usually appear in organic search results. Featured snippets are elements designed specifically for devices that have little space for search results. Google created Featured Snippets. For this reason, webmasters cannot influence them. Website designers, however, can influence their development a little by using structured data. Experts advise you to test exactly for which search queries the featured snippets appear. Depending on the result display, webmasters should then give improved responses to reach the zero position (which is the featured snippet location). Featured snippets are mainly the result of what or how questions. For this reason, it is worth using keyword finders and keyword explorers to find suitable keywords.

❹   Adapt website contents for the local search

The local page adjustment is absolutely necessary for the verbal search. Therefore, correct, current and complete local data must be provided to the virtual assistants. Consistent use of data such as address, contact number and company name is also essential. As already explained in the chapter "Local SEO", the use of industry entries such as Google My Business is worthwhile so that the companies for the search queries "near me" do not remain undiscovered. Furthermore, the maintenance of the topicality of the entries is a necessary condition.

⑤   To recognize the intentions of the users

Recognizing the user's intentions is an important ability to take first place in the verbal search. For this reason, a precise anticipation of the user's questions is indispensable. Furthermore, webmasters must know what the user's intention is with the search query. As soon as the intention and the corresponding question are clear, the web designers should start with the construction of the appropriate answers. The "Answer the Public" tool is best suited for this purpose, in order to determine which questions users ask in connection with certain key terms.

⑥   Use spoken language

The contents should correspond to the language style of the verbal search queries and be reproduced in a natural tone. In addition, the texts are written in such a way that they can be easily read aloud. That is why tactics like keyword stuffing are out of place. In this respect, it is worth talking to customer service. The employees know which questions the customers ask most frequently. Webmasters can then create a FAQ list from these and, based on this list, create FAQ pages that precisely answer the most important customer queries. This also increases the probability of appearing in a Featured Snippet.

⑦   Use Longtail Keywords

With regard to the verbal language search a Longtail Keywords optimization is worthwhile. As a rule, these terms contain complete keyword phrases that come very close to the spoken language. They also address a targeted group of users.

However, it should be mentioned at this point that the keywords of the speech search differ from the written keywords. The keywords that have priority for targeting are keywords that originate from a natural language. As already mentioned, they contain longer search terms. These usually include five or even more words. According to previous studies, these are usually whole question sentences. The sentence "Definition of online marketing" should provide an answer to the question "What is online marketing like? Meanwhile the keywords, which are relevant for questions, can differ. For example, users can ask the question "How does link building work?" while the language search answers the question "How can I create additional links to my domain? Users can find the relevant keywords in all search tools. Google even displays them as a possible suggestion. Site operators can use third-party tools to find matching keywords. AnswerThePublic.com or Ubersugget have proven to be useful tools in practice. Those who are looking for questions that customers actually ask. As already mentioned, a detailed consultation with the customer and information center is worthwhile. Try out a live chat is becoming increasingly popular as customers can immediately ask an employee about their problems and difficulties. Using a live chat test phase, webmasters can form relevant questions that they use in their speech search engine optimization.

4.3

INSTRUCTIONS FOR OPTIMIZING CONTENT FOR SPEECH SEARCHES

As soon as the keywords that are important for the language search have been found, webmasters can start optimizing their page content. One advantage of optimizing the language search is a better structure of the presented content. Google, on the other hand, prefers well structured content.

1 Selection of topics

First, the webmasters must select a topic and create the appropriate content with the most frequently asked questions. Similarly, they provide answers to these questions regarding the brand, product and service. The contents should definitely answer the questions "Who, what, when, why, where and how". Webmasters who approach topic selection in this way can easily add the identified keywords. The focus of their language optimization is on weaving these keywords into the presented page content. SEO experts know that it makes little sense to optimize language expressions, since less than two percent of the respective voice results contain the exact keywords in the title tag. That is why webmasters should optimize their pages as they usually do and add as many questions as possible. However, these should be similar to speech expressions.

2 Structure answers in a targeted way

The longtail keywords mentioned are the best measure with regard to the questions asked and the associated website content. The general guideline is not to exceed the 30 word limit. According to studies, Google answers questions with a maximum of 29 words. However, the guide value is not mandatory, but merely a recommendation. Google also provides shorter or longer answers as needed. The following example illustrates this situation. The answer to the question: "Which is the longest season?" contains 30 terms. "Do bee stings hurt?" Even contains 50 words as an answer. Experts recommend that you take a test and enter your questions in Google before you start. This enables companies to analyze the responses of their competitors. Competitive analysis is a popular tool in marketing for maintaining or even improving your company's status.

❸ Optimization of content for forms

When creating the long form content, webmasters should integrate as many answers as possible. This allows them to benefit from a better ranking position. However, the keywords should of course be embedded in the content. Depending on the nature of the keyword, these can also be integrated into the headings and subheadings.

❹ Briefly design the content for language optimization

Webmasters can also create a short concise content that puts a high focus on the keywords. For language optimization, it is recommended to concentrate on the FAQ list. The content should be structured according to a set of key terms for questions. Subsequently, webmasters add additional keywords to their designed answers, which are not typical question keywords. The chapter on "Domain Authority" deals with this tactic in more detail.

❺ Perform an optimization for the featured snippets

SEO experts believe that 40.7 percent of linguistic search results come from featured snippets. By optimizing the featured snippets, webmasters can increase the likelihood that their content will appear in the voice search. In order to optimize the featured snippets in the best possible way, website designers should use structured data. Depending on the content type, a schema markup is used. For example, those who answer the question "How can I change oil in my car?" should use the "HowToSection" mark in the code of the web page to help Google to identify the relevant data when browsing the content. When using schema markup, webmasters should ensure that content is optimally structured using headers, clear enumerations, and numbered lists. This makes it easier for Google to filter out and present the relevant answers to users' queries.

⑥ Create content with a natural language

As explained in detail at the beginning of this chapter, the speech search scores with its natural sound. The language that is entered via the keyboard sounds unnatural and artificial. The principle of natural spelling has top priority. Webmasters who answer the question "How to find out if a mango is ripe" will do themselves a favor if they create a content match that Google can easily find. In this context, the answer Google found was: "If the flesh under the skin yields slightly at the touch of a finger, the mango is ripe". The most helpful tip for optimizing content in speech search is to include as many longtail keywords, including question keywords, as possible. Such an approach can result in a single Web page being considered relevant for a large number of different language search queries.

4.4

LANGUAGE SEARCH ADVICE FOR LOCAL
SEARCH ENGINE OPTIMIZATION

The possibilities that SEO experts have for capturing local customers using linguistic search optimization are very exciting. However, there are some aspects that webmasters have to take into account when searching locally as well as in the corresponding voice output. The majority of users tend to look for a company by asking the following question: "Cosmetic shop New York". In answering this question, Google relies on the website content available. Still, the question "Cosmetics shop near me" searches Google for a shop that is close to the user. Google uses Google My Business Profiles (GMB) to locate the closest possible company. Webmasters should take these little things into account when optimizing them. They should not only optimize their content for general inquiries, but also for those who will claim the Google My Business profile with their question. The entry in Google My Business also ensures the correct company data such as name, address and telephone number. In addition, entrepreneurs can use this function to categorize their organization. Cosmeticians who categorize their profile as a beauty salon increase the likelihood of appearing high up in the results when someone is looking for a "beauty salon near me".

① More Advice and Strategies for a Successful Voice SEO

There are other aspects that webmasters should consider if they want to increase the frequency with which their site appears as a result. The following advice is intended as an orientation for improvement with regard to language search.

② The brand should be included in the Knowledge Graph

The more data Google has at its disposal, the more likely it is to appear in the Knowledge-Graph panel. The relevant data includes the company name, the website and the target group. A structured markup helps to achieve this goal. It is also worth actively operating social media company profiles and subsequently linking them to the brand. This gives Google even stronger signals. A Wikipedia page can help here. These often appear in the search result pages for language queries. They are particularly popular for general knowledge questions.

③ The pursuit of a reading level of 9th grade has already proved itself in practice several times - Effortless and clear wording is generally a good directive. SEO experts have found that content that matches the wording of a 9th grade textbook is displayed much more often than language search results. A special Flesch-Kincaid rating indicates to which category the content can be assigned. A value of 9.3 indicates that the content of the reading level of the 9th grade. Webmasters have the possibility to control their content in advance. The tool named "readable.io" displays a note rating after inserting a text.

④ An increase in domain authority pays off in any case

Websites that contain numerous links referring to themselves appear much more frequently in organic searches than their competitors. The same principle applies to the verbal search.

⑤ Videos in search results are considered extremely helpful

Videos make up a large part of Google's strategy for answering linguistic questions. They tend to appear more frequently when using natural keywords. When a user performs a standard search for "cook artichoke", Google knows that the user is interested in preparing an artichoke. Thus, webmasters set the associated videos as a third result after their respective text snippet or the questions asked by users. When web page designers use a keyword in a natural language, such as "How do I cook an artichoke?", the video snippet appears at the top. Such snippets start with the relevant part of their video that answers the specific request. However, there are cases where Google displays the response to the description in the box rather than the video. Webmasters should aim to rate their videos by making them for good search engine optimization. To do this, they must optimize their titles and write detailed descriptions of their videos, which contain the natural keywords.

6 **A fast loading time of the page is indispensable also with regard to the speech search** - In July 2018, Google announced that it had introduced a so-called speed update for all users. Because the loading time is an important ranking factor for the mobile search, webmasters should improve this when designing their own website. An average search results page of the language search loads in about half the time that the average traditional pages take. The side speed is enormously important to capture the Featured Snipppet cutout.

7 **The website must be mobile friendly**
Since Google launched Mobile First Indexing, the condition of a mobile friendly website has been a significant factor in website ranking. In the meantime, the majority of individuals mainly use voice searches on their mobile phones. That is why webmasters have to optimize their website to land in the featured snippet. For that reason Google has introduced a test that evaluates usability for mobile devices. This test allows webmasters to see if they need to optimize their site for mobile devices or not.

THE FURTHER DEVELOPMENT OF THE LANGUAGE SEARCH

Experts attach great importance not only to the intention of the users, but also to the mood of the users. They also emphasize the importance of monetarizing the language search for companies. Podcasts were among the contents that are enjoying increasing popularity in the area of voice search. But also recipes and news have found their way into the language search. Because of this development, Google has created a clever directory called Google Assistant Actions. This provides an overview of actions that are enabled thanks to the numerous search commands of the Google Assistant and through which the content is found on selected pages. Furthermore, webmasters can check the mentioned "actions" pages of their content, change the information provided at any time. You also have the option of setting the visibility of the content.

The verbal search is still in its infancy. However, experts expect a strong further development in the coming years. For this reason, clever webmasters are already looking for these potentials today. Furthermore, it is worth starting with the optimization for the language search. The relevance of the featured snippets should be in the foreground. A precise answering of customer and user inquiries increases the success of the language search. Companies that optimize their websites for local, mobile and voice search are well on the way to meeting the demands of the future in terms of Internet usage.

Conclusion

Basically, verbal search engine optimization does not differ much from conventional SEO. Ultimately, Voice SEO represents a new standard for exquisite and high-quality optimization methods. The positive trend of language development is becoming more and more important.

 Tip:

Do not forget your free SEO-Analysis for further information.
Get it now **www.seomarkt.de/premium**
Password: **SEO2019DE89**

Content Marketing and the Relationship between Search Engine Optimization

5.0

C ontent marketing is a marketing approach that does not use advertising messages, but produces meaningful content that numerous people search for online. An exact analysis of this marketing instrument, however, also proves how closely content marketing is linked to search engine optimization. Content marketing as well as good SEO measures are aimed at a defined target group. Therefore, organizations combine content marketing with a well thought-out SEO strategy to present valuable content with the help of a customer journey. Companies that provide content along the customer journey are found much more often than their competitors. In addition, they strengthen a company's ability to trust and thus benefit from winning new customers. As a rule, the Buyer Journey takes place on digital platforms. The Customer or Buyer Journey represents the complete purchase process of the customer. Thanks to this process, companies have the opportunity to meet potential customers with their content marketing. However, content marketing has a useful content that strengthens the basis of trust and is also closely related to search engine optimization. Furthermore, the majority of Internet users are annoyed by all advertising measures. Users therefore rely on Adblocker. In addition, movie fans enjoy broadcasts on Netflix because this platform is ad-free. Users use the Internet to find out about a product or service before making a purchase. Website operators should always keep in mind that content marketing is closely related to search engine optimization. In order to realize an effective content marketing, which helps to reach a higher position, the choice of keywords and the right ON-Page search engine optimization and technical SEO is extremely important.

5.1

THE CONCEPT AND OBJECTIVES OF CONTENT MARKETING

The following definition of content marketing comes from the Content Marketing Institute:

„Content marketing is a strategic marketing approach focused on creating and distributing valuable, relevant, and consistent content to attract and retain a clearly-defined audience — and, ultimately, to drive profitable customer action."

Content marketing pursues several goals. "Strategic marketing Approach" stands for the existence of a plan, the definition of goals and the development of procedures to achieve the set goals. Moreover, content marketing is not a tactic like running social media channels, blogging or a regular email marketing policy. It is a strategy that includes the elements of social media and lead generation. The latter represents the sales opportunities. Further goals of content marketing are the creation and distribution of valuable, relevant and consistent content. However, this requires a content process. Professional editors who are of the respective subject and have a command of the desired target language are absolutely essential. Meetings in editorial offices and with people who are very familiar with search engine optimization are part of this task. Content formats consist of blog articles, videos or whitepapers. Other goals that companies want to achieve with content marketing are to attract and maintain a clearly defined audience. This goal poses a real challenge, as the majority produces content that does not appeal to the target audience at all. Content strategists and clever tools can provide a real remedy when taking the right path. Another goal of content marketing is to promote profitable customer campaigns. After all, the maximization of turnover is the first priority of a company and this can only be achieved with a presentable and continuously increasing profit. If the goal is also customer loyalty, the adaptation of processes such as good customer care is mandatory.

5.2

MATCHING CONTENT IS THE BIGGEST CHALLENGE

According to surveys, marketing content creators regard the creation of suitable content as the greatest challenge. This is due to the limited resources of suitable journalists, which companies usually have at their disposal in order to produce an appealing content for the target group. Content must be characterized by the property "very good", otherwise the desired target group will not find it. This in turn does not mean that leads are achieved. Companies usually have to write between two and three blog posts per week to provide their customers with up-to-date content. It should also contain at least 700 words. Videos and whitepapers also belong to a good and appealing content. The following instructions serve as orientation for the creation of a successful content.

Instructions for creating a successful content

1. The first question that companies should ask themselves is the nature of the website. This should receive a large number of visitors. Good content cannot help maximize sales if it is overlooked by search engines.

2. Target groups represent another aspect that is indispensable for content marketing. That is why companies need to know their target audience well in order to produce and publish appealing content. Content marketing is not a means to produce links that only please Google. Before companies start producing content marketing, they think about what their target audience is interested in. Customer service, which answers frequently asked questions, can serve as an important support. Content marketing only reaches users if it really appeals to them. In online shops, marketing and sales experts talk about so-called buyers or user personas. These are prototypes of the respective user or target group. They depict fictional customers. However, the data on which the figure is based is real. They are made up of sociodemographic characteristics, needs, actions and online buying behavior. The construction of the buyer user can be very helpful for creating an appealing content marketing. It is therefore worthwhile to draw up a list of questions and then answer them.

✓ What are the sociodemographic characteristics of the Buyer Persona?
✓ What is the persona's position in the world of work and what is a typical working day of this user like?
✓ What are the personal and professional goals of this persona?
✓ What are the personal and professional challenges?
✓ Is it an Internet-savvy persona who also makes online purchasing decisions?
✓ Does the use of social networks belong to this persona?
✓ Does the persona use the Internet to obtain information about the desired product?
✓ Which aspects lead the persona on the day of the purchase decision to make the respective purchase?
✓ What exactly is necessary to convince the persona of the particular offer or service to purchase?
✓ Does the persona make the decision entirely alone or does she involve other users in the alternative?

3. Are there good copywriters or editors who can write good content? As companies provide good content several times a week, they need a team of good and motivated authors. But content strategists are just as important. They are constantly developing the content strategy further. In order to score with a successful content, copywriters start with a topic that was answered neither by the competition nor by other websites. Finding market gaps has always been a success factor in the free economy. Those looking for an unknown topic can expect to offer added value to their users. It also gives them a significant advantage over their competitors. The first step is to find several topics. In the second course, subtopics are derived. These ideally contain important keywords as well as relevant keywords. It is also worth answering the classic W questions, which were explained in detail in the chapter "Search engine optimized texts". However, Google Suggest is also a useful tool for creating successful content. After the preparation of a list with the relevant questions and keywords the control takes place. The authors check which search results Google displays for the terms mentioned. Clever copywriters go through them step by step and take notes. They collect important sources, expert opinions and relevant studies. The number of hits can range from ten to fifty. For this reason, the points that offer users added value are filtered. Another good side effect resulting from this approach is the study of competitors. This allows companies to better match what their competitors specialize in. Customer surveys are also part of creating good content. Because the interest of the users is definitely the focus of attention. This procedure helps to produce clear sections of text. Text deserts cannot occur at all thanks to this method. Loose text structures are created with the help of matching images, enumerations and subheadings. But even the best copywriters need feedback in order to convince with good articles. This is due to the high probability of quickly losing track of the essentials. Authors are usually very absorbed in a topic. That is why they need qualified feedback. This is the only way they can determine whether they are repeating themselves in the course of the text or have not mentioned an important point. Neutral readers are best placed to judge whether the text is written comprehensibly for outsiders. Experts in the field are better able to confirm whether the red thread is adhered to throughout the text. Authors cannot judge the question of suitable graphics and important sources entirely on their own. They also need feedback on these aspects.

Finally, the critical questioning of the text determines the success of the content. A sufficient investment of time, effort and diligence is part of content marketing. Readers immediately notice whether or not the authors wanted to offer them added value with what they wrote.

4. Is the existing budget sufficient to promote the desired content? W h e n the production of content marketing is fresh, Google's traffic is too low to be successful. Companies must advertise. The easiest way to do this is via social media channels such as Facebook, LinkedIn, Xing, Twitter or Instagram.

5. Are all relevant tools available?
   Digital support is the be-all and end-all for content creation. The copywriters need good tools, especially for optimization. They can either use several individual tools or a single powerful marketing automation software. In addition, the employees must also be familiar with the respective tools.

5.3

MEASURING AND MONITORING THE SUCCESS OF CONTENT MARKETING

In marketing, managers pursue goals that are measurable, objective and reliable. The advantage of online marketing is the ability to measure these goals. In the following, the most important figures that content producers should consider at the beginning of their creation are explained.

1. Visits: How many users visit the website and which sources did they use? Was it through Google, a social media channel or a newsletter? Thanks to the Google Analytics tool, content producers can determine the number of visitors.

2. Social media users on social media platforms: a change has prohibited a direct addressing of users, therefore content producers who directly address users of social media channels have to make a financial effort. For this reason, it is worth switching to free alternatives.

3. Newsletter and blog subscribers provide the crucial indication of a regular connection. They prove how important the presented content is to them. They also provide an incentive for content marketing producers to regularly formulate fresh content.

4. Lead generation: leads stand for visitors who were interested in further content and downloaded personal data for it. They represent an attractive group as subscribers. Because these visitors have expressed their interest in a selected content and given the website operator their express consent to contact him for further sales targets.

5. Marketing qualified and sales leads: This is a class of leads that tend to or have concluded a purchase.

6. Sales and closing determination: Even if the sales department does this, marketing professionals are also careful to obtain these figures, otherwise they would never be able to prove the positive return on investment of their marketing methods.

7. Other relevant key figures: Among the key figures worth mentioning are click-through rates, e-mail opening and conversion rates for landing pages.

Conclusion Content Marketing

Since the Customer Journey takes place predominantly on digital platforms, both marketing and sales activities of a company must become digital. Online content marketing has overtaken classical advertising, as the majority of consumers avoid conventional advertising measures. Useful content consisting of blog posts and videos is very popular, unlike advertising.

Tip:

Do not forget your free SEO-Analysis for further information.
Get it now **www.seomarkt.de/premium**
Password: **SEO2019DE89**

The role of social media for better marketing in the context of search engine optimization

6.0

M arketing is a business area that must constantly adapt to the latest technologies in order for the respective company to successfully assert itself in the market against the competition. The social media have long been known for their role in marketing, but many companies still do not use them. Many executives do not even know how high the impact of social media is on organic search results. Social networks also function as search engines. Accordingly, social media strategies are unprofitable without a well thought-out search engine optimization.

6.1

DEFINITION OF SOCIAL MEDIA MARKETING

Social Media Marketing stands for all marketing activities that take place on social media platforms. This includes numerous campaigns that include the social media aspect. Writing a blog article, conducting a restructuring campaign or using Facebook, Twitter and Instagram stands for active social media marketing. The webmasters do not apply any new or even unique tactics. They simply adapt to the new marketing requirements. In addition, marketers aim to increase their brand awareness and value. They want to win the trust of potential customers and at the same time increase their authority. Increased traffic on your website is just as much a goal as the intention to turn website visitors into customers. However, the highest priority of marketers is to meet customer needs. After all, they ensure the continued existence of the company. For these reasons, a combination of social media and search engine optimization strategies is worthwhile.

Although the social signals do not flow directly into Google's search algorithm, the use of social media can still improve the ranking and increase the audience's reach. Social signals play an important role in this process. They consist of communicative and informative signals. These in turn establish social relationships through social interactions and emotions. In practice, these are reflected in the famous like, share or comment functions. The signals mentioned help with the evaluation of the respective social media channel. With regard to search engine optimization, experts speak of social signals when interactions arise on the social media platforms with the help of interactions. A share of a web page on Instagram is a classic example of this context.

Webmasters should be aware of the connection between the social signals and the ranking. Sound studies prove that websites that appear in the upper positions of the search result pages have an above-average number of social signals. Analysts found that websites with numerous social signals reflect the online presence of a famous brand. Furthermore, they are characterized by a large amount of current content. However, experts have still not been able to prove whether the social signals actually have both an active and a passive effect on a ranking.

Google employees also point out that search engines have difficulty indexing the huge databases of social networks such as Facebook. Nevertheless, they confirm the importance of social signals, which will increase in importance in the near future. Google employees also stress that social platform websites do not enjoy special status and are treated in the same way as other homepages. However, experts continue to argue about the relationship between social signals and their importance for search engine optimization and ranking. Google has not confirmed whether social signals serve as ranking factors. Nevertheless, marketing experts regard social signals as an important instrument of online marketing. After all, Likes and Shares can increase the range of the audience within a few minutes many times over. Therefore it is obvious that social signals will eventually find their way to the ranking criteria.

Still, social signals can provide search engines with clues as to whether the content of a website is in demand among users or not. At the same time, likes and shares act as important indicators of current search trends and topics. In addition, since May 2015, Twitter social platform tweets have been appearing in Google's organic search results. Webmasters can also use Google Analytics to evaluate social network traffic.

6.2

IS THE USE OF SOCIAL MEDIA MARKETING WORTHWILE IN TERMS OF SEARCH ENGINE OPTIMIZATION?

For the majority of companies, organizations and firms, social media marketing is now a matter of course. With these platforms you can increase your reach many times over. Furthermore, many companies argue that the use of social media channels is free of charge. However, this is not the case, because

Internet-savvy employees invest a lot of time to position the company correctly in the social media channels. And time is money. Moreover, social media marketing does not work the same for every company. Furthermore, it is not a tool to achieve a high turnover within the shortest time and with little effort. The main reason for using social media platforms is the great potential of the channels. The results depend on the chosen strategies. But the list of advantages offered by social platforms is long. On the one hand, companies can offer fast customer service and it does not matter where the customers are located. On the other hand, companies enjoy the opportunity to sell their products and services in new ways. In addition, companies can benefit from a joint development of loyalty and brand perception. Furthermore, companies can advertise new products without having to invest a large part of their budget in many advertising measures. The following instructions can be consulted both by companies that still want to gain a foothold on the social media platforms and by companies that have long been represented on the numerous channels. They also learn how to combine SEO and social media in a meaningful way.

A good start defines success

Strategists define a list of goals they want to achieve through social media activities. The activity on the platforms also depends on the products and services offered by the company. Economically oriented companies and charities pursue conflicting goals and therefore proceed differently in their activities. Whether a company is non-profit or economically oriented, however, plays a subordinate role for the search engine ranking. Search engines search and index the content of both organizations equally. Company profiles appear in the organic search results. The following examples illustrate the differences between a for-profit and a non-profit company and explain what it takes to score points in search engine optimization. The economically oriented company called "Product GmbH" achieves a high turnover with the sale of products in numerous department stores. Since the products enjoy a high level of awareness, Product GmbH benefits organically from a large number of followers on the social media channels, although it is not particularly active on these. Now the company decides to win the followers for an increase in sales by introducing online sales and new products. Product GmbH makes online advertising for the new offers. A clear strategy can be derived from these objectives.

- ✓ Social media representatives now have to post information about the new products at regular intervals to promote sales.
- ✓ A targeted switching of paid online campaigns increases the number of followers and sales equally.
- ✓ Clever strategists animate followers who are already using the advertised products to win more followers who will also be convinced by the offers.
- ✓ Competitions and promotions tailored to social media channels do not contain the same content as traditional printed brochures. They contain a short product description and brief testimonials from enthusiastic users.
- ✓ Good content that is popular with followers and enjoys frequent sharing is also indexed faster by search engines. Therefore it is worthwhile to pursue the goal, which consists in a large number of Likes.

A nonprofit organization like the World Wide Fund for Nature (WWF) benefits from a high profile as it has conducted great offline PR campaigns and TV commercials. However, until recently they had no social media activities and therefore had to start from scratch. Their aim is to increase awareness of environmental and animal problems, to advertise events, to receive donations and to win new members. In this case, there are several ways to achieve these objectives. However, they must make their site publicly visible and use the relevant keywords to increase their success. These settings have a strong effect on the search results.

- ✓ WWF can use the channels and promote them through other media. These include e-mails, posts, links in TV commercials or on the website. In this way, the organization can quickly increase the number of followers. But marketing managers need to create separable and emotional content in order to spread the message organically and attract new followers. The choice of keywords therefore plays a decisive role.
- ✓ Non-profit organizations basically pursue a similar objective as economically oriented companies. They are also interested in increasing the number of followers. However, they would like to raise more money to continue their fight against environmental disasters and the extinction of endangered species. WWF aims to raise public awareness of the environmental and species problems that have fatal consequences such as global warming and flooding. WWF has several options for this project.
- ✓ You can use the channels and advertise them through other media such as e-mail, mail, links in TV commercials and on their websites to quickly increase the number of followers.

✓ Furthermore, the WWF can use divisible and appealing content, which at the same time awakens deep emotions among followers and potential followers. In this way, the WWF spreads the message organically and attracts a lot of attention. Baby dolphins or elephants killed or pictures of indigenous peoples who have to give up their habitat due to a deforested rainforest usually appeal to the emotions of the viewer. In this way, the WWF can benefit from higher donations. However, you must add the appropriate keywords to your images.

The two examples illustrate how two completely different companies proceed in order to realize the number of followers via social media platforms and the desired corporate and organizational goals. Nevertheless, companies should beware of using black hat techniques.

The following aspects of action represent a recommendation for supporters who wish to practice social media marketing.

Checking the stand for social media and a meaningful link to local search engine optimization

Those who already actively operate social media should check their status. Companies that have not yet created a page can start from scratch. Regardless of their current position, organizations should monitor which channels they are active on. A comparison between the channels is worthwhile in every respect. Some social media sites are better suited to certain businesses than other platforms. With its breathtaking and emotional images, WWF is now better off on Instagram than on Facebook. Staffing providers who want to attract new customers and applicants will be more successful with their activities on Xing, LinkedIn or Facebook than on Twitter or Instagram. An analysis of the current audience is never wrong, as the turnover or donations depend on it. A restructuring of the content is also recommended.

However, companies should add a so-called geotag to their mail. In this way they combine SEO with social media. Furthermore, the location of the company in the business profile is a must, because it increases the probability of being found in the local SEO. In addition, this is an ideal way to differentiate a company from the competition. The advertisements are to be individualized both by postcode and by city name. The action prompt called "Plan your route" or "Call now" increases not only your ranking in search engines, but also the likelihood that customers will actually take action. Even on social media, a company profile can be created with the most popular online directory called Yelp.

① Creating a positive brand image

Well-known Google employees have confirmed in interviews how important the view of followers of a certain brand can be for the ranking. According to them, entrepreneurs should use every lever to promote positive mentions of their brand on social channels as well as in forums.

② Creating strategic partnerships

The majority of entrepreneurs continue to pursue the first strategy in their social media strategies, which consists of a systematic dissemination of content in social media. However, social networks can also serve to build strategic relationships from which real partnerships can develop. To create a partnership, however, three steps are necessary.

✓ Brand fans

Brand lovers are nothing more than active users who have shared and liked the content. They have positively spread the brand name in the social media. Active users of social media channels multiply the effectiveness of a corporate brand free of charge.

✓ Organic Influencers

Organic influencers are different from paid influencers. Organic influencers are profiles of users who have an influence on the brand thanks to their acquired expertise. They also have authority and a high level of trustworthiness. Their positive distributions also have a corresponding effect on the audience.

✓ Strategic Partners

Strategic partners represent profiles for non-competitive organizations or influential personalities in the respective industry. They serve the creation of meaningful contents and the exchange of experiences, which give both partners an advantage.

Due to the high role that social media platforms play in the everyday lives of numerous companies and private individuals, the majority of companies find that operating on channels pays off in every respect. They can reach a larger audience and thus increase their turnover. Internationally active companies such as L´Oreal Cosmetics, Nestlé or the car brand BMW should always create a company page in English on the social platforms due to their worldwide reputation. They owe that to their worldwide customers.

 Tip:

Do not forget your free SEO-Analysis for further information.
Get it now **www.seomarkt.de/premium**
Password: **SEO2019DE89**

Measuring and demonstrating the success of SEO

7.0

n order to measure the success of SEO, companies need to know their Key Performance Indicators (KPI). These are key metrics used by online marketing professionals to measure and prove the success of a website. Continuous monitoring of the key figures is a measure to ensure success.

Webmasters who know the performance they have achieved and who observe and subsequently evaluate the search engine optimized data according to a defined scheme are in a position to effectively manage their SEO measures. This increases traffic and conversions. This chapter describes in detail which KPIs people who deal with SEO should have in mind. When searching for suitable indicators, it is worthwhile to re-visit the goals pursued by search engine optimization and what it stands for. SEO measures stand for all the efforts that webmasters make to improve the visibility of a website in the search engines and thus achieve a good ranking in the free search results and regularly attract new visitors. Rankings are the first step in a presentation of the order in which success is monitored. The impressions and then the clicks follow. These are on the same level as the traffic. After the traffic comes the interaction. Finally follow the conversions.

7.1

DISPLAY OF THE TRAFFIC CHANNEL

On- and off-page efforts are aimed at positioning website content that can be indexed by search engines as high as possible using relevant keywords. This statement shows that SEO fulfils the role of a traffic supplier. The Google analysis proves this connection. It provides webmasters with search analysis metrics such as rankings, impressions and clicks. Experienced web administrators include the results of the Google Search Console in the rating. It provides a good overview of the status and development of click rates and impressions of a URL.

Traffic loves conversions

Still, profound and indisputable SEO does not end with the topic "traffic", but focuses on the complete process of users and their behavior. They all flow into the control of the SEO efforts. Websites can only be successful in the long run if they meet the expectations of their users. In addition, the traffic presented must take into account the most important corporate goals and conversions. Google Analytics is a useful tool to understand this conversion tunnel. The following key figures belong to the data that should be taken into account in a search engine optimized success control:

Visits (page views)

The Visits index stands for the organic visitors from the various search engines. This KPI represents the connection element to the clicks from the Google Search Console already displayed. However, the data are by no means 100% analogous to each other.

In addition, multiple Adclicks can result in a single visit. This is the reason for a difference. In order for a new visit to be recorded, the last visit to the website must have taken place a little while back. Users must be able to be clearly separated so that different visits can be registered. Furthermore, visitors often stop visiting the website before a visit has been recorded. The advertising medium is nevertheless entered. This phenomenon is often a side effect of websites that are characterized by a particularly long loading time. Moreover, the counting pulse of the tracking on the respective landing page has not yet been triggered. Nevertheless, deviations between clicks and visits are unavoidable. It is therefore worthwhile to carefully set up the associated tracking tools and to take a close look at the analysis and the results obtained from it.

Bounce Rate & Time on Site (bounce rate and dwell time)

Depending on the objective of the content or the page variant, user metrics such as the bounce rate and the time spent on site act as good indicators of whether users really found what they were looking for. Experts define a jump as the visit to a single subpage of an online presence. Google Analytics refers to a jump as a visit to a single landing page, whereupon the website is left without further visits or queries to the server being triggered. A bounce rate

thus consists of visits to a single page, which is then divided by all sessions.
It represents the percentage of sessions on a web page where visitors only click on one page and only send a single request to the server. Furthermore, the duration of such visits shall be 0 seconds.

However, whether a high bounce rate is a bad sign depends on various factors. If the success of a website requires several individual pages to be called up, the bounce rate is a bad sign for such an online presence. This is particularly true for news articles, product pages and payment transactions.

Nevertheless, if the respective website is a single page like a blog, the high bounce rate is not a bad sign, because no further page visits are to be expected.

Conversion Rate and Sales (Conversion Rate and Revenue)

SEO traffic can only be evaluated in monetary terms if the conversion targets can be evaluated. At this point, however, the attribution model used plays an important role. Because when comparing the key figures with other marketing channels, an internal benchmark can be achieved. The conversion rate plays a key role here. It is a measure when online shops want to determine the success of affiliate campaigns as well as the effect of their keyword marketing. In addition, the conversion rate reflects a known phenomenon. It proves that despite an extensive marketing campaign, the number of site visitors is increasing, but there is still no increase in new customer registrations. The conversion rate explains the causes of this phenomenon. It can also measure the impact of advertising measures. Web designers or companies that carry out advertising measures find out how many clicks in a percentage have led to a corresponding customer campaign. This is followed by a detailed breakdown into macro and micro conversion rates. In the case of an online shop, according to this subdivision, a product order counts as part of the macro conversion rate, whereas clicking on the corresponding banner falls into the category of the micro conversion rate. This results in an overlap of the terms click-through rate and micro-conversion rate. In this way, the conversion rate is proportional to the total number of visitors. This in turn drives the success of the advertising campaign.

In marketing, the conversion rate acts as a turnover and conversion rate. Since it mainly serves as a control instrument for online marketing activities, it occurs mainly in the context of marketing. The conversion rate determines how many website visitors become product or service consumers. It also defines how many visitors have made a lead. The conversion rate is calculated using the following formula:

$$\text{Conversion Rate} = \frac{Total\ Transactions\ (with\ website)}{Total\ Visits} * 100$$

The calculation returns a result in a percentage value. Where a higher percentage value is considered more positive than a lower digit. However, the formula is a generalization as it does not include the number of repeat visitors. In order to correct this falsification of results, the unique visitors must be consulted. Accordingly, the modified formula is as follows:

$$\text{Conversion Rate} = \frac{Count\ of\ Transactions\ by\ Unique\ Visitor}{Count\ of\ Visits\ by\ Unique\ Visitor} * 100$$

The following example serves for a better understanding and clarification of the connection. This is an online shop that produces handmade shoes. In order to determine whether recent marketing activities have achieved their corresponding effect, the owners of the conversion rate of the website are presented with the following data:

$$\text{Conversion Rate} = \frac{100}{500} * 100$$

The result delivers a conversion rate of two percent, which is positive for a company of this size.

Cost-per-Acquisition (CPA)

If the website operators have left the costs per marketing channel in the advertising analysis, cost-per-acquisition can also be a valuable indicator that helps to assess the SEO success. Cost-per-Acquisition defines the ratio of the costs used to achieve a conversion target. At this point, benchmarking with other marketing channels is worthwhile.

7.2

A LOOK BEHIND THE SCENES ON SEARCH ENGINE OPTIMIZATION

With regard to checking success, everything starts with ranking when it comes to search engine optimization. But the secret of success lies in the detail. For this reason, a detailed presentation of the ranking and the associated key figures is provided, which must be taken into account in search engine optimized reporting and monitoring. The rankings and visibility are directly related. Basically, the Google Search Console provides a good insight into the rankings of your own website. It acts as a free source of relevant data. The problem is the existence of the data format. In the form in which the data is available, an evaluation turns out to be rather complicated. That is why many webmasters make use of a further and individual keyword tracking via various Internet tools. In addition, it is worth taking a look at the competition (a so-called competition analysis) for search engine optimized monitoring. Relying on the Google Search Console is not enough to check your SEO success. To create a good overall picture of the performance of the respective key terms, it is worth displaying a visibility index. Different tool providers such as Sistrix or Searchmetrics can help. With their index number, they represent a generic impression of how the ranking developed from the selected period in comparison to the competition. There are areas for which the tools mentioned can be of importance, even if the ranking data used were not determined by the user. Those who leave the so-called black box cannot avoid defining their own keyword set. You can calculate your own visibility from this. Numerous tool providers allow good solutions.

THE SIGNIFICANCE OF OFF PAGE KEY

Backlinks are still among the most important ranking factors. For this reason, it is worth observing the development of domain popularity. However, a quantitative evaluation of incoming links does not represent a useful statement about the actual condition of the backlinks. Rather, the quality of the backlinks is important. Therefore Domain Authority (DA), SpamScore, Trustflow and Page Authority (PA) have to be checked.

If the analysis of the domain popularity reveals any discrepancies, it is worthwhile to conduct a detailed analysis. Experienced SEO experts therefore monitor both their own domain popularity and that of their competitors.

Search queries for a selected brand

Backlinks are not the only important aspect in the offpage area. The level of brand awareness is also a decisive factor. Companies that manage to realize a higher demand achieve corresponding advantages in the ranking. Search engines reveal brand search queries of users and their concerns. Google can easily determine how often searchers have typed a brand name into the search bar alone or in conjunction with other keywords. This indicator plays an important role in SEO monitoring. For this reason, the Google Search Console can display clicks and impressions data by both generic and brand-related keywords. That is why website analysts document brand and non-brand keyword clicks and impressions in a separate chart within their SEO performance reports.

In addition, a documentation about brand awareness and a comparison with the competition based on the search volume data of Google AdWords and Keyword Planners makes an enormous contribution to the improvement of the website ranking.

Crawling Errors and Statistics

Google's crawling statistics show how often and with what kind of performance the Google Bot crawled the respective URL in the selected period. If there are special fluctuations, an exact log file check should be carried out as a measure. In addition, the Google Search Console shows which errors or other difficulties the Google Bot had to overcome during crawling. Accordingly, regular monitoring of these indicators helps to improve the ranking of the website if the problems described are identified and eliminated using appropriate methods. For this reason, these key figures should not be missing in a complete search engine optimized reporting.

Clicks and traffic - a clean separation of data

When the analysis of the clicks in the Google Search Console search analysis files ends, the traffic of the organic search in Google Analytics starts. Many beginners suspect that the amount of clicks is comparable to the traffic data. However, this is not the case. Limitations exist for data entry. Tracking data can only be included in Google Analytics if the matching code is always perfectly integrated. If this is specified at the end of a text, but the website visitor clicks rather on another link and leaves the page for this reason, this page visit can no longer be counted. In addition, blocking JavaScript and using other tools, such as browser add-ons to disable Google Analytics, and can block the recording of user traffic. Furthermore, Google Analytics relies on a clear instruction. In practice, it often happens that sections of the SEA traffic are counted to the SEO channel. This is due to a missing link from Google AdWords to the Google Analytics account. However, other incorrect settings may also be responsible for this. If there is a wide gap between Google Analytics and the Google Search Console, it is worth checking this aspect out. For privacy reasons, Google does not collect and display all data in the Google Search Console. Search queries that users rarely perform are not taken into account. Inquiries containing personal data or confidential information will also not be considered.

Various measurements and processing of the relevant data

The basic definition for the data calculation is different for each tool. Google Search Console statistics can differ from other sources because each tool rates bots differently.

The tools do not follow the same procedure when evaluating the restrictions of search results or automatically removing duplicates.

The following example illustrates an automatic removal of a search entry in the Google search engine:

In order for you to get only the most relevant results, several entries that are very similar to the 99 displayed hits have been removed. However, if you wish, you can repeat your search by taking the skipped results into account.

Or:

Some results have most likely been removed due to the provisions of European data protection law. Further information...

 Tip:

Do not forget your free SEO-Analysis for further information.
Get it now **www.seomarkt.de/premium**
Password: **SEO2019DE89**

Representation of Black Hat SEO

8.0

B lack hat SEO stands for an illegal approach that some webmasters use to achieve a better website ranking in the search results. You are breaking the rules. However, this unethical method is punished by the search engines. The well-known Black Hat tactics include keyword stuffing, cloaking and the use of private link networks (PBN). For a company, appearing in search results is essential. The emergence promotes the growth of the company and thus also of turnover. But as with so many things in life, there is both wrong and right way to perform search engine optimization. The dark side of the black hat SEO is definitely the undesirable possibility. Black Hat SEO is eager to search for search engine algorithms instead of solving them for the respective users. This tactic does not deserve the right to appear as high up in search results as possible, but instead uses questionable methods to launch the web pages into the upper ranks. Accordingly, the use of Black Hat SEO techniques damages a website and thus the company. The Internet presence is thereby deteriorated and not improved.

Those for whom the subject of search engine optimization is an unknown terrain should keep in mind the goal of a successful SEO. The intent of search engines like Google is to present optimal results when users perform a search. They also want to ensure that users have an excellent search experience that is free of all spam. The search engines use an automatic technique. Their algorithms pursue the goal of recognizing Black Hat SEO actions and then punishing them. Due to the progress of search engine algorithms, it is no longer worth practicing Black Hat SEO. Instead, webmasters should focus on the white hat SEO, the methods of which are explained in detail in this book. This is a better alternative to a successful search engine optimization. White-Hat-SEO takes into account the prescribed rules.

BLACK HAT SEO TECHNIQUES

The term keyword stuffing is known to people who deal with search engine optimization. In this method, website operators use irrelevant keywords to influence their ranking in search results pages. However, the users punish this procedure. They are not interested in different keyword versions that do not offer them any added value. Furthermore, such pages fall under the heading irrelevant queries. According to Google, keyword stuffing means creating phone lists without any added value, creating meaningless text blocks, and repeating words or phrases until they sound artificial. The following example stands for a typical keyword stuffing on the subject of electrical household appliances:

> "We sell electrical household appliances. We sell electrical household appliances. If you are looking for electrical household appliances, please contact us. In case you need new electrical household appliances, ask one of our electrical household appliance department consultants."

Google recognizes that this content not only sounds unnatural, but also represents a keyword stuffing and thus punishes the ranking of the website.

Cloaking - A Black Hat SEO Technique

When cloaking, webmasters create different content. They do not show their users the same part of the content as the search engines. Websites that use Black Hat SEO thus aim to prioritize page content for a large number of terms that are meaningless to their content. Websites that act as spam websites often use this technology. In this way, you want to prevent a search engine bot from discovering the spam content. Because then it can no longer be displayed to the users. However, an adaptation of website content to different user groups is permitted. This includes reducing the size of an online presence when users of mobile devices access it. Automatic language adjustments are also acceptable. This means that if someone accesses the site from Spain, they are allowed to view the Spanish version.

Use sneaky redirects

Redirects imply sending people or domains from websites other than those on which users clicked. Black Hat SEO does not use redirects for the purpose for which they were created. Redirecting highly authoritative websites with numerous backlinks to meaningless sites to improve rank in search results is also one of the unethical black hat SEO techniques. 301-forwardings redirect the vast majority of authority from one website to another online presence. Thus, webmasters who exercise Black Hat SEO only use redirects to edit their search results. However, redirects should only be used for the purpose for which they were created. This applies in particular to a change in the website domain or a consolidation of two contents. Furthermore, on selected occasions, webmasters can use JavaScripts to redirect website visitors. This can happen with a Xing profile. In this case a logged-in user would see the complete profile if it is not blocked. Whereas Xing users who are not logged in to Google can only watch a public version of a profile. Sneaky redirects, on the other hand, are an absolute taboo as they definitely violate the Google search engine guidelines.

Offer content of inferior quality

Content that is characterized by inferior quality and offers no added value to users is a typical Black Hat SEO element. Bad content is content that has been copied from a competing website, bot or other person. There were gaps in search engine optimization that prevented Google from recognizing copied web page content. But in 2011, a so-called panda update eliminated this difficulty. Once upon a time, the majority of websites with duplicate content were extremely popular in search rankings. But since Google has evolved into the discovery of duplicate content, the search engine can easily detect both inferior and duplicate content. Furthermore, the weaving of invisible keywords into the page content is not permitted. Website operators who practice Black Hat SEO integrate invisible keywords in the same color as the website background into the texts. Accordingly, the obfuscated keywords can be displayed even if no visible content is visible on the respective page. Users who then click on the search result and believe that they have found the topic being looked up will be disappointed. Unfortunately, you cannot find the content you are looking for because the keywords are hidden. High bounce rates ultimately result from inappropriate content.

Those who prefer their users should not have to hide the content of their website. Furthermore the bait and the switch belong to the other illegal black means to falsify the results in the search engines. With this goal, webmasters create a content that relates to a topic for which they want to realize a high ranking position. However, as soon as the pages appear in the search results, the webmasters exchange the content for another one. Still, users are annoyed by this deceitful bait technology. While this approach attracts users and search engines alike, it should be avoided as it is not a good way for a successful SEO.

The creation of high-quality content, on the other hand, stands for good white-hat SEO tactics. It is not only necessary to avoid a punitive measure, but also to delimit the Internet presence. Accordingly, select content ensures that the respective target group builds trust. Furthermore, a carefully selected content transforms page visitors into customers.

Misuse of structured data

Structured data is also known as rich snippets. At this point, webmasters have the opportunity to redesign the ads of their website content on the result pages of Google and other search engines. This approach creates a unique selling point and gives the website designers more space on the result pages. Thanks to this method, you can integrate structured data into a page that includes a podcast, a recipe and numerous offers and services.

Characteristic for Black Hat SEO is the provision of inaccurate content in the structured data for Google and other search engines. Webmasters who operate Black Hat SEO rate themselves or their products and services with five stars from adulterated rating sites. They then add structured data to emphasize it on the search results pages. This method is extremely risky and is almost always uncovered and punished. Google asks its users to report websites that are suspected of misuse of data. This fact should not dissuade a conscientious webmaster, however, from marking true and exact content on their online presence. Those who provide truthful information do not need to worry.

Leave spam comments in blogs

The headline points out that with this black hat SEO technique, instead of leaving comments with added value, webmasters prefer to place a link to their website. However, web designers can no longer easily get through with this tactic, as the majority of search engines, including Google, have updated their algorithms. This prevents them from using the link function in blog comments. The majority of blogs contain links that lead to blog comments. Accordingly, search engines do not follow the given link. In addition, the left link does not pass through any authority. Furthermore, the link specification in blog comments belongs to a spam method that conscientious webmasters should refrain from. Those who have a forum, community, or blog that includes a comment feature should regularly check whether the comment area has been sent by bots or other people. Not only Google, but also other search engines like Yahoo or Bing remove web pages that contain spam content after a check.

Linkfarm - a deceitful Black Hat SEO tactic

Link farms are a collection of web pages that only pursue the goal of creating links. Each individual website is linked to the homepage or the Internet presence that appears high up in the search engines. Search engines classify pages into a specific category by using the number of existing links referring to the web page as a benchmark. Black Hat SEO takes advantage of this process by using link farms to consciously increase the number of backlinks on a homepage. Link farms are often characterized by inferior quality content and numerous links. These usually contain a keyword for which the page should have a certain position in the anchor text. Since good search engines like Google can find link farms without any difficulty, webmasters should refrain from practicing this black hat SEO technique. Those who use white-hat SEO instead are better off.

A rewarding white-hat SEO technique is to create amazing content that offers users real added value. This is described with explanatory diagrams, well-researched data, high-quality interviews and other content that allows a natural back link acquisition.

Using private blog networks

Private Blog Networks (PBN) stand for a series of authoritative web series that merely pursue the goal of link building. Each PBN website is linked to a different page, which would like to assist it with the search results. Black hat SEOs that aim to build a private network typically purchase expired URLs, but have enjoyed a certain authority status. They then compose a content that was present on the website before the domain expired and then add links to their page. They assume that search engines do not reveal the control of their self-made website network and instead rate their homepage many times higher in the search results. But now search engines even recognize private blog networks (PBN). Therefore, webmasters who use this Black Hat search engine optimization technique must expect a penalty. Consequently, it is worth focusing on creating a unique content. Marketing experts prefer to create an umbrella brand. This means that website operators who keep their content under one roof benefit from a highly authoritative website, as a large number of users link to this domain.

8.2

REASONS THAT SPEAK IN FAVOR OF AVOIDING BLACK HAT SEO

Even though Black Hat SEO is not one of the illegal practices, it still violates the webmaster guidelines that have determined search engines. In the end, it is still a violation of the rules. Therefore, webmasters who apply Black Hat SEO must reckon with a sanction that is detrimental to their home page. If a penalty is imposed, the rank of the website in the search results also drops. In the worst case, it is completely erased. The result is then lower traffic and a reduction in the number of customers, which in turn leads to a drop in sales. Since the creators of the search engines continuously improve them, Black Hat SEO users can almost no longer trick them. Black Hat SEO does not provide any added value to users or search engines. Although some webmasters have seen a short-term increase in profits thanks to Black Hat SEO techniques, they have suffered a bitter blow of removing or deactivating their site.

The blurred boundary of Grey Hat SEO

Techniques that are neither black hat SEO nor white hat SEO are grey hat SEO practices. These are composed of questionable SEO techniques. The search engines have not expressly prohibited these practices, but they are not recommended and could therefore be banned in the near future. The trend that grey techniques of search engine optimization are declared to be black illicit practices continues unceasingly. Therefore, webmasters should exercise caution when applying Grey Hat SEO techniques.

Advice on how to effectively avoid black hat SEO techniques

There is no tool that can refute the fact that black hat SEO is a risky and loss-making tactic. Furthermore, removing the website from search results is sufficient proof of how pointless and ineffective the black techniques of search engine optimization really are. Therefore, in the following, so-called "Best Practices" are presented which help to avoid Black Hat SEO techniques.

✓ Webmasters should treat website visitors and search engines in the same way and stop cloaking or tricking search engine crawlers by directing them to other websites.

✓ The goal of the webmasters was to focus on proposing solutions for visitors and creating a flawless user experience from the search engine to the online presence.

✓ Qualitatively selected texts that are free of any keyword stuffing increase the success factor. Scratching, cribbing or rephrasing content belonging to another author does not add value for users or webmasters. Therefore, it is worth considering content policies before webmasters publish their site.

✓ The compliance with the rules when weaving the structured data to the website ensures the success factor.

✓ It is recommended to ensure that the supplementary marking of the scheme does not mislead the user.

✓ Creating private blog networks to increase the number of links is a tab measure.

✓ It is worth creating a unique website that attracts users with its excellent content, rather than faking, copying or rewriting it without adding further information.

✓ Regularly looking up the guidelines for webmasters helps website designers to stay up to date without unwittingly practicing black hat SEO techniques.

The focus, however, is not on clarifying the question: "How can I successfully escape a Google punishment? If webmasters have to ask themselves whether their approach is consistent with Black Hat SEO techniques, they can assume that this is the case. That is why white hat SEO strategies are a better approach. This approach pays off in the long term. Webmasters do not have to fear any punishment or even removal of their site. Avoiding Black Hat SEO techniques is therefore worthwhile in every respect.

Tip:

Do not forget your free SEO-Analysis for further information.
Get it now **www.seomarkt.de/premium**
Password: **SEO2019DE89**

Ranking algorithm of Amazon and the Amazon search engine optimization

9.0

T he following chapter is dedicated to the crucial functionality of the Amazon Ranking Algorithm. However, there is no presentation of the individual measures necessary to optimize Amazon's ranking. Nevertheless, merchants and sellers who are looking to optimize their sales rank on the Amazon sales platform can use this chapter to expand their knowledge horizons. Users who can understand the aspects of Amazon's ranking algorithm and its important relationships are also able to create their ideas and marketing strategies to optimize an Amazon bestseller rank. The following hints can be used as a guide for the Amazon SEO area.

9.1

PRODUCTS THAT ARE AT THE TOP ARE THE WINNERS

Experts have confirmed that the majority of Amazon customers use traditional searches to find suitable products. The other buyers get to the offers thanks to external links, bestseller lists or filters. Users only view the results on the first page. A minority clicks through to page three. The percentage of users who even click further is extremely low. Accordingly, the same secret of success applies to the Amazon sales platform as it does to Google. Companies that appear at the top usually emerge as winners from the search.

Amazon follows the principle of presenting users with products that they are most likely to purchase.

Amazon is eager to make as many purchases as possible on the platform. Because the company enjoys a commission for every sale made. Therefore, a user must click on at least one product on the results pages after completing a search and then buy it in order for Amazon to successfully complete its plan. This is why Amazon is interested in presenting users with offers that are precisely tailored to their needs. Amazon uses two steps to realize this plan. Step one is the filtration of the appropriate products. The offers are then sorted and arranged. An automatic ranking algorithm in turn determines the arrangement.

Filtration of suitable products (1st step)

On Amazon.de, users can purchase more than 100 million products. This number is rising continuously. Still, users express their interest only in a small selection of the products presented. With the help of a search query they expect the display of the requested products. Amazon is responsible for a successful interpretation of the inquiry and the selection of the subset of the assortment. To make the right choice, Amazon uses two criteria. For a start the products found must contain the search terms entered. During the selection process, Amazon uses different information fields of the product such as title, bullets, description, keywords, brand, dealer name and other product information such as color. If a user is looking for a red leather rucksack with silver rivets, the displayed offer must contain the keywords red, leather rucksack, rivets and silver. Amazon, however, leaves specific filler words like with and in out of the search process. Amazon ignores the difference between upper and lower case. Singular and plural differences are also not taken into account by the sales platform. The search terms only have to be present in the same information field. For this reason, dealers include their offers with an extensive set of important search terms. In particular, they go deeper into the special features and extras of the products. But not only the keywords, but also the main image is indispensable for a good search result. The main picture shows the complete product without going into any details. In this image, users see the entire product and not just part or a section of it.

Sorting of suitable products according to their purchase probability (2nd step)

After the filtration of the content, the products are presented by means of a ranking. This creates a better overview thanks to a list consisting of several pages. In addition, thanks to the sales rank, Amazon can display the offers that users find fastest. The ranking algorithm determines the order in which the products are positioned. It considers different product characteristics, weights them and then assigns a position to the offer, which determines the relative ranking in the list. As already mentioned in the previous section, Amazon aims to generate as many purchases as possible with its ranking. If the ranking is well presented, customers benefit from a fast settlement process. This is why Amazon arranges its products according to the probability of purchase. For these, however, two factors must be taken into account. The first group of factors is called performance factors. They represent the desired performance of the offer and are recorded with metrics such as the click rate, conversion rate and the sales made.

So-called relevance factors represent the second group of relevant factors. You determine how well an offer matches a search query. Keywords are the key factor for determining relevance factors. In this way, Amazon presents users with products that have benefited from a high level of sales success in the past and are highly relevant to the content of the search query. The higher it is, the higher the sales. A high sales volume implies a better commission for Amazon. Amazon Ranking Optimization requires retailers to increase their relevance by using important keywords. Attractive product conditions and presentations have a positive effect on the likelihood of purchase. The focus is on the keywords, because these increase the decision-making pleasure. For this reason, it is worth optimizing the relevance with regard to the keywords. The following chapter describes the performance and relevance factors.

Performance factors focus on proven and successful products

Products that have stood out in the past for their flawless performance benefit from a better ranking position. After all, these represent a higher purchase probability. At Amazon, the term performance includes the three key figures:

- ✓ sales
- ✓ click rate
- ✓ conversion rate

In the sales analysis, popular products in particular have proven themselves, as these articles encourage further customers to buy.

High-selling products not only benefit from a high ranking position, but also from a bestseller ranking in their respective product category. In order to understand the meaning of the click rate and conversion rate, it is necessary to illustrate the purchase process at Amazon. After the first step of a user, which consists in the search query, the click of the product takes place, in order to realize a forwarding to the product page. However, the purchase requires another click. These two steps are measured using the click rate and conversion rate. The click rate reflects the frequency with which users click on a product. A frequent click represents a high product attractiveness. Products that are often displayed but hardly ever clicked on symbolize a low degree of attractiveness. Offers that users do not click are never bought. The purchase probability is therefore 0 percent. By contrast, products that are often clicked on also benefit from a higher sales rank, as clicking on them increases the likelihood of purchase. However, products do not have a general click-through rate. This depends on the keywords and the ranking. A pocket benefits from a higher click rate with the keyword "pocket" than with the keyword "mobile phone". Furthermore, a product in first place achieves a much higher click-through rate than a product that is only in 34th place. The click rate is therefore determined on the basis of a keyword and ranking specification. If the model of Michael Kors has a low click rate in the keyword "designer lady bag" at number one than the "designer bag" of Armani at number one, then the Armani handbag will stand over the Michael Kors version. The principle is simple: the higher the click rate of a product for a specific keyword, the higher the sales rank at Amazon.

The conversion rate, on the other hand, is responsible for measuring product purchase. It shows the number of purchases after the users have inspected the product page and purchased the respective offer. Products that regularly encourage customers to buy are very popular among customers. Products that are never purchased, on the other hand, either do not contain any relevant information or contain information that prevents users from making a purchase. Bad reviews are sometimes a common reason against purchasing the product in question. High conversion rates represent a high purchase probability. For this reason, these products are higher up the list. Analogous to the click rate, the conversion rate also varies with the selection of keywords. The latter also acts as a means of controlling the click rate. If this is extremely high for a certain keyword, but the associated conversion rate is very low, this indicates a lack of interest on the part of users as soon as they take a closer look at the product. If a bag has the title Michael Kors, the picture is such a bag and the price is only 35 Euros, the users will click on the product. If, on the other hand, the product description states that the bag is an imitation, only a small number of users will purchase the bag. This results in a low conversion rate.

If there is a wide gap between click rate and conversion rate, this speaks against the information provided. They are either incomplete or have raised false expectations. Such products experience a decline in the ranking. Performance factors serve as an important valuation tool for product purchases. Online merchants are not interested in presenting products that are characterized by a poor sales rate. Amazon does not receive any commission for unsold products.

Retailers can positively influence the performance factors with a successful product presentation and accommodating product conditions.

For retailers, the crucial question is how they can influence these factors. However, you should know that a direct influence on the conversion rate, click rate and sales is not possible. However, sellers and merchants have almost all the components that encourage users to click and buy an offer. You can adapt and vary the necessary components according to customer requirements. Thus, they can provoke a higher click rate and conversion rate, which in turn increase sales. Traders must achieve their goal through an indirect approach. In order to determine which factors the merchants have an influence on, a high capacity for empathy, which requires a transfer into the situation of the buyers, is necessary. The question of which information or product descriptions users use to make a purchase represents the core of the analysis.
The following list provides a clear overview of the relevant factors.

✓ The title contains popular search terms. (Example: designer bag Michael Kors)
✓ An appealing image has a positive influence on the perception of customers.
✓ The brand is not only clearly mentioned in the title, but also in the description.
✓ In addition, the price is clearly and visibly displayed. Among other things, it forms the basis for a purchase decision.
✓ It should also be mentioned whether Prime customers benefit from fast delivery.
✓ Availability is also important as it is an important purchasing Reviews are not negligible, because customers read them carefully before clicking the Buy button.

✓ The bestseller label is an important decision factor that can increase the likelihood of purchase.
✓ The delivery costs must also not be missing, many users often decide against a purchase if they are too high or choose another product to qualify for free shipping.
✓ A marking of the product category also belongs to it.
✓ Other offers are important but play a subordinate role.

Dealers can largely influence these factors. However, the brand, the bestseller label and the product evaluation cannot be influenced. A so-called heatmap suggests that the selected image is the most relevant decision criterion. But also the information on the left side such as the title, brand, price or availability enjoy a high status. The rating, on the other hand, receives less attention on the search results page. Traders should only internalize the importance of the title and the image as these have a big influence on the click rate. For this reason, it is worthwhile to rotate the images and test how the choice of image affects the ranking and click rate. With regard to price, users orientate themselves on relative prices. You compare the lower and higher product prices to find out to which price class your chosen product belongs. Positive ratings in the four and five star range as well as the bestseller label can also have an affirmative influence on the click rate.

Users who click on a product are then redirected to the product pages. In this step, merchants aim to maximize their conversion rate. Here, too, everything revolves around the question of which factors motivate Amazon members to make a purchase decision. In the analysis of this question, putting the customer in the position has proven to be extremely helpful. In contrast to the search results page, retailers place additional images, information, descriptions and ratings on the product page, which they can influence. The field called "Customers who bought this item also bought...". The arrangement allows an authentic prioritization of the information fields. In order to read the product description, users must skip certain fields. Reviews can be found at the bottom of the product page. If the image corresponds to the user's taste, the probability of a purchase increases. However, if the images are not appealing, the user will leave the site and look around the search results page for other products that are more in line with their wishes. Since both the pictures and the bullets sometimes decide on the purchase, their special attention is worthwhile. Detailed product information should always be available because it can particularly motivate indecisive buyers to make a purchase decision.

Clever traders also turn their attention to the valuations. They apply "the Japanese doctrine of failure". They concentrate on the negative evaluations and react immediately to them. In this way, they signal to their buyers that they are taking a serious approach and taking their complaints seriously. They can also explain at this point what measures they have taken to avoid a repetition of the aspect complained about.

At the conversion rate, merchants benefit from significant opportunities that can assist them in exerting an affirmative influence. With regard to the information fields, sellers and traders must comply with certain formal aspects. You should use at least five bullets and include images with over 1,000 x 1,000 pixels in the description. Pixel compliance is mandatory to enable a zoom function. When it comes to content, it is worthwhile to test different types of information. Some merchants are wise enough to check which effects increase the conversion rate. It may be the case that the addition of a single bullet character contributes to a significant increase in the conversion rate. If the sellers of expensive women's handbags add that the leather is genuine, this can be the last impulse that encourages bag-enthusiastic women to make a purchase.

Factors influencing the conversion rate the performance factors explained have a strong impact on the ranking. With the help of the product presentation and the associated product conditions, the salespeople can exert a partially large influence on the important performance factors. However, the actors must determine the contents on their own. Experienced online merchants recommend making changes as part of test runs and observing their effects over a certain period of time. Traders should focus on the ranking changes. The so-called Marketplace Analytics analysis platform can provide an enormous remedy for this procedure.

Relevance factors provide important clues

Relevance factors are an important part of the Amazon Ranking Algorithm. The performance factors reflect the sales rate of a product, whereas the relevance factors measure how well the content of an article matches the user inquiry. The relevance is determined using the key terms. Dealers are pleased about this connection, because they can choose the keywords themselves. Accordingly, they enjoy full influence on the relevance factors.

Keywords and their role in determining relevance

Amazon filters out all articles that do not contain all the keywords from the query after a search query has been carried out. During filtration, Amazon takes into account the content of information fields such as title, bullets, product information, description, search term, vendor, and brand. However, not only the presence of the search terms plays an important role in the ranking, but also the order in which they appear. Since each individual information field receives a different weighting for the ranking, it does not matter in which field the respective keyword is located. Keywords that are already included in the title definitely promote the ranking. In second place, however, are the enumeration points, the keywords used and additional product specifications. It is worth integrating the keywords into the product title, as they help to achieve a better ranking. Furthermore, the match between the search query and the product keywords used is extremely important. At best, the search terms are all placed in the same order in a single information field. If this is not the case, the relevance drops many times over. So if a lady is looking for "black handbag by Armani", a bag that has the terms "black handbag Armani" in the title will be preferred by users rather than a product that cannot prove these terms in the title. Nevertheless, traders should know which descriptions increase relevance. Short titles and bullets are among the factors that not only increase relevance, but also have a positive influence. If the title of an article consists of the term "fitness bands" and that of another product consists of the words "Beautiful bands that can also be used as fitness bands for yoga training", the first article with shorter title will be more relevant. Similar to search engine optimization for a domain, merchants active on the Amazon platform face the same challenge in terms of ranking optimization. You must first find the appropriate keywords and then decide in which information field and in which order you want to enter them.

Relationship between relevance and performance factors

The mentioned relevance and performance factors jointly determine the ranking of an article in the search result by incorporating them into the ranking algorithm. However, this process does not take place in isolation from each other, but under mutual influence. Some of them work in the same direction. Matching keywords contribute to an increase in the click rate. Nevertheless, the two factors also work in different directions. From the perspective of the keywords, it would be worthwhile to enter a majority of the keywords in the article title and in the bullets of the product offered. Still, the performance perspective speaks against this method, as users click on long titles much less often. Therefore, a holistic consideration of the performance and relevance factors is necessary in order to prevent a mutual negative impact of the two factors on each other.

Enhanced Brand Content - Another Important Factor in Amazon Search Engine Optimization

Dealers who sell well-known brands benefit from so-called Enhanced Brand Content (EBC). Moreover, the sellers can only use this if they have registered a trademark and at the same time registered with Amazon. While using the EBC, merchants may use additional images. This step focuses on a better brand presentation. Those who effectively structure Enhanced Brand Content and provide it with an appealing design not only increase the trust of their buyers, but also increase their conversion rate. With regard to the images,

dealers should know and apply the difference between the main image and the additional images. Because the main picture only allows a representation of the core product, the use of a white background and a capture of the picture at a rate of 85 percent. The additional pictures, on the other hand, allow the illustration of the accessories as well as the packaging, a brief presentation of the backgrounds and details, props and instructions for use. In addition, the additional images can be used to present good text, schematics and sketches.

OPTIMIZE AMAZON FOR THE USE OF MOBILE DEVICES

Online retailers are recording a rapid increase in sales, which is gaining in importance on the use of smartphones and tablets every day. In the meantime, numerous customers are buying their favourite products via mobile devices. The proportion of buyers who carry out their purchases of mobile terminals is constantly increasing. In 2016, the share of mobile traffic was 38 percent, whereas in 2015 it was only 29 percent. The development for mobile sales is similar and also represents such a high increase. Amazon is not immune to this mobile shopping trend either. The Amazon Shopping App proves this fact. It has been downloaded over 50 million times by users of mobile devices. For this reason, Amazon merchants must also present their articles in the mobile view as well as in the shopping app in the best possible way for their customers and thus encourage them to buy. The optimization of Amazon articles for mobile devices is responsible for this. It increases mobile traffic and the number of products sold. The effort to improve mobile performance is therefore worthwhile in many respects. In addition, improved mobile performance provides better ranking on both mobile devices and the desktop.

Significant differences between Amazon Desktop and Amazon Mobile

Those who use mobile shopping via Amazon usually use two types of devices. They use either the tablet or their smartphone. The tablet view is only slightly different from the desktop view. With regard to the smartphone, however, there are important distinguishing features that require explanation. In general, smartphone versions have inferior information content with shorter text. The page structure corresponds to the smaller view on the mobile phones. Even the smartphone has other special features, because users can access Amazon either via their mobile smartphone browser or via the Amazon Shopping App. The latter is a restrictive view that offers users a reduced version of the product presentation. Nevertheless, the basic rule is that a completely isolated optimization of the mobile and desktop versions is not possible. Both the mobile and desktop versions use the information provided in the backend of the respective article. Therefore, the challenge is to display the mobile view coherently with the desktop display. Since the display in the Amazon Shopping App is restrictive, it can serve as an orientation for the desktop display. So the goal is a successful display of the app. Experts point to nine significant differences between the desktop display and the shopping app.

Shorter titles

The titles must be shorter in the shopping app, as only the first 70 characters of the respective title are displayed in the mobile display of the search results. This gives rise to the question of what such an optimization best looks like. The first rule is not to waste any characters. It is therefore worth mentioning an important product advantage in the title, as this increases the click rate. An example for the representation of hiking boots would be: "Robust and weatherproof hiking boots". In the desktop version, the title could be a little longer and read as follows: "Lico Milan Men's trekking and hiking boots waterproof, non-slip, breathable and windproof".

The only description is "above the fold."

With the mobile variant, "above the fold" the text field to be described is only permitted for the longer variants. The bullets, which contain important product information, can only be found below in the mobile version. After a successful and informative title design, an appealing image is selected to attract the user to the respective product. The features and benefits that make this product so unique are already high on the list, as customers can only get more information by scrolling through the product description.

The pictures are smaller

Product images are much smaller in the mobile display. This rule applies in particular to search results. Since the article images are displayed much smaller in the mobile version, they must be easily recognizable for an optimal click and conversion rate. When choosing the image for mobile devices, a good detail is extremely important, as it strongly influences the purchase decision. The exemption also plays an important role. Because the white background puts the product in the focus of attention.

Number of images shrinks from nine to seven in the mobile version

In the mobile version, the first seven images are displayed on the respective product page, regardless of how many photos the dealers have uploaded. With the mobile version, the buyer can actually only take a closer look at the first seven images. For this reason, dealers should take great care to select only the most important images. Accordingly, these seven images must contain detail images, accessories and certificates. Only then can they have an influence on the conversion rate.

Fewer bullets

Dealers must also be brief with the bullets. In the mobile version, customers only see three of the five bullet points. The other two can only be viewed by the buyer after clicking on the detailed view. Still, the first three bullets are displayed in their total length without any abbreviations. That is why it is worthwhile to show the most important bullet points at the top. This allows merchants to achieve a better conversion rate.

Product description with the aid of bullets

The description of the mobile devices is given directly above. A single glance is all it takes to read them, as bullet points represent them succinctly. In the desktop version, the description is placed further down and below the bullet points. Due to its positioning, the description in the mobile version benefits from greater significance. It thus has a similar effect to bullet points in terms of the conversion rate. Therefore, a convincing article description is essential for the mobile version. Thanks to the block positioning together with the bullets, merchants can benefit from even better conversion rate effects if there is a good complement between the two elements.

The first 200 characters are decisive

The teaser text shows only the first 200 characters. It also does not contain HTML formatting. Headings or approaches are misplaced here. Only after a further click can the dealers use the HTML formatting in the detailed view. The basic rule of a teaser text also applies to the mobile Amazon version. The teaser contains the most important product information that motivates the reader to read on. Since no HTML formatting is allowed here, the title should nicely go over to the first sentence of the product description and merge with it.

Only the three best ratings are displayed

Mobile product pages show only the three best ratings. Amazon concentrates on reviews that other users have marked as particularly helpful. Nevertheless, the site visitors can view the other ratings with a further click. Since initial ratings are critical to first impressions, traders should disregard negative reviews and focus instead on positive feedback from buyers. Due to the low number of reviews, merchants must be careful to select the best and most informative reviews.

Comments on the reviews are not displayed

Both buyers and sellers have the opportunity to respond to reviews. In the mobile version, however, the comments are not displayed. Negative ratings are important because, on the one hand, they increase the reality factor and, on the other hand, they give dealers the opportunity to react to them and thus prove to customers how seriously they are actually taken by sellers. But with the mobile version, merchants do not have the opportunity to present their answers, as they are simply not displayed there. For this reason, the information that the merchants merely convey through comments should also reach mobile users. Therefore the use of the question and answer area is worthwhile.

Enrich search engine optimization with AI - provide insight, automation and personalization

10.0

Technology giants have discovered the trend called "AI-first", where AI stands for Artificial Intelligence. Dealers and marketers who use this principle significantly improve their search engine optimization strategies. One of the founders of this strategy, Jim Yu, focuses on three core areas of marketing.

Google has made worldwide headlines with the presentation of its new Duplex. This is a high-quality artificial intelligence system (AI) that communicates with humans in a natural language. People can use this system to schedule a hairdresser appointment or reserve a table at their favourite restaurant. The AI systems differ in a certain way to pass the Turing test, but these differences are irrelevant to users. Google Duplex has proven to many enthusiasts how well it can do this test. But according to experts, this system is only the beginning of a future potential. AI systems benefit from global headlines because mankind has always been fascinated by such applications. People love AI systems that mimic interpersonal interactions. However, the development of AI systems is also comes with disadvantages. Many people fear losing their jobs as a result of the systems. Marketers view this development process from two angles. AI either takes over a large part of the work or complements and expands people's capabilities. Digital translation machines have not replaced translators, because people who rely on the translation of a document need a stamp of a sworn and certified translator. But the translation equipment has made the work of translators and interpreters much easier. You no longer have to rely on thick dictionaries, but can look up the word you are looking for within seconds. This shortens your translation time many times over. However, translation is not the only category that makes people's work easier. The list of categories in which AI systems complement human capabilities is long. A study by business magazine Economist found that 75 percent of executives value the potential of AI and are therefore interested in expanding and actively implementing it in their company. The high number represents the credibility of this project. When this hype is translated into reality, it becomes clear that the second positive perspective is the conceivable result. This result would also be desirable, as the company's auditors, PricewaterhouseCoopers, predicts that AI will contribute 15.7 billion US dollars to global GDP each year by 2030. This development together with the number provides evidence of an endorsement of the AI systems.

AI is now present in all areas. It is embedded in products that people use on a daily basis. This includes Swarovski as well as Netflix. Marketers know how deeply AI is integrated into a search. In addition, it opens up a wealth of additional opportunities for SEO experts. AI systems also play an important role in the search. They make them more human in a paradoxical way, thanks to the interactions involved. Although the search is not yet able to communicate with users as the Google Duplex demo has shown, its goal is to enable such a search in the near future. Google's Rank Brain technology uses machine learning to comprehend and understand the presented content it crawls. The system derives the intention from search queries that are characterized by ambiguity. It also uses feedback data to improve the accuracy of the results. Thus the system listens to the people and acquires a new knowledge in this way. Even if people do not always have an overview of these processes, they can obviously examine the results. There are now 37 search result pages (SERP). But this figure represents the beginning of a new era and it will evolve in the near future.

Even if the potential for personalization is still in its infancy, a Google employee named Sundar Pichai has confirmed this fact. He also noted that the age of the "AI-First" company has arrived. For this reason, it is worthwhile for companies to adapt to this search landscape. After all, AI works on many Google products. These include the Google Photos and Google Lens system. One of the co-founders of artificial intelligence systems made the statement that AI now affects almost every major project. The pace of development in this field continues to develop at a rapid pace. Google has found that AI offers users useful and better results. The user satisfaction factor increases thanks to the AI. Search marketers are forced to include these technological advances in their offers if they want to use these opportunities for a successful SEO.

LINKING SEARCH ENGINE OPTIMIZATION WITH
ARTIFICAL INTELLIGENCE

In practice, there are three core areas in which AI can contribute to improving SEO performance. They consist of the areas of automation, personalization and insight. In the insights, artificial intelligence processes and interprets a certain data pattern on a scale. People would never be able to do that. Such replication is impossible for the human brain. This valuable addition is seen by search strategists as beneficial because it enables the AI to provide information on which people depend to make basic decisions from unstructured data. However, analysis is one of the most popular areas in which search engine optimization can support AI. The important analysis areas include market trend, location and competition analyses. AI also supports access to customer intention reports. Pay-per-click spend management and SERP performance also benefit from the development of AI systems. These open up new horizons in the areas mentioned, which would have gone unnoticed without their existence. Because the traditional search goes beyond the traditional search result page and has meanwhile developed into a multidisciplinary channel, it is becoming increasingly important. Novel development trends, such as visual searches, play a key role in artificial intelligence. In addition, it fights its way through as a sensible alternative when processing other types of media. The social media platform called Pinterest makes use of this learning and thus interprets the content and context of images. Accordingly, the trade has numerous further opportunities to use the "discovery search".

Google Lens focuses on the extended reality. The tool aims to merge the physical world with the real world. It uses objects as questionnaires instead of typical keywords. Of course, this development process will lead to a data creation of an priceless value. Each interaction reveals a novelty about the respective audience. Marketers aim to use AI to ensure that they capture, manage and use their data correctly. Furthermore, they achieve better effects in the development of search strategies. To use artificial intelligence for SEO insights, webmasters need to understand the basic needs of their customers. An identification of the possibilities of the content is indispensable. Furthermore, the CI can help to define market gaps in the competitive analysis. KI also helps with the investment of long-term content. AI also helps ensure that the content presented is easily searched and displayed by all users.

Search engine optimization is a labor-intensive field, which requires gigantic attention in the long run. Still, if there is a way to automate tasks to generate the same output of information, realizing that opportunity, should be a top priority. The valuable time gained thanks to the automation process can be wonderfully applied to disciplines that require human skills more urgently. These include the creation of strategy and creative content. The following tasks represent a possibility for automation in search engine optimization.

Advice for starting search engine optimized automation with the help of artificial intelligence

- ✓ Technical audits are excellent automation processes for search engine optimization.
- ✓ Keyword searches can also be automated and would effectively support the work of SEO strategists, as would electronic online dictionaries supporting translators and interpreters.
- ✓ Content optimization and content distribution can also benefit from the AI.
- ✓ Tag management and internal linking will make SEO strategists' work easier in the near future.

In the case studies mentioned, while computers can replace human labor, professionals will continue to have control over tasks and logical decision-making. Thanks to AI, SEO experts can use their time for more demanding search engine optimization tasks.

1. In practice, it has proved helpful to divide the tasks to be completed into smaller subtasks. However, an assessment of the automation potential of the tasks on a scale of zero to ten is indispensable.
2. The use of a rule-based automation process to execute uncomplicated, yet time-consuming jobs has proven particularly effective in practice.
3. A good balance between human activity and automation is a good basis for the use of artificial intelligence.
4. Using ML algorithms and the appropriate data quality or quantity to increase performance with AI is a sensible move.
5. A focus on improving the user experience and speed monitoring makes sense in any case.

THE PERSONALIZATION PROCESS

Thanks to personalization, marketers are able to create significant and meaningful moments for each individual customer. But this task requires technological support. AI is an essential part of this process. Amazon has been the market leader in personalization for a long time. The online retailer uses user data and their historical purchases to suggest new and interesting items to its customers. Amazon uses this method to advertise products that are not immediately visible to everyone.

The mentioned approaches are a helpful support for SEO strategists. Thanks to the allocation of the content to different intentions of the users, new sales possibilities arise. These solutions exceed the conventional search engine optimization many times over. The trend is confirmed several times in the latest Google developments. The integration of the Assistant into Google Maps provides proof of this development.

Meanwhile the content search is not only limited to search result pages. For this reason, sellers and providers of additional services must really understand their customers and their needs in order to be able to contact them at any time. In this step, artificial intelligence is of crucial importance. The area called Predictive Analytics helps create predictions based on historical data and behavioral patterns to shape future content to meet consumer needs. This raises the question of how artificial intelligence can be used in SEO personalization. The following list provides possible ideas.

✓ The creation of content according to Persona, Customer Journey or a special delivery mechanism is a suitable option for personalization.

✓ An improvement of the user experience as well as a conversion with a targeted personalization are possible and recommendable.

✓ Semantically specific pages are a good way to link user requests and intentions.

✓ The use of well-structured personalization and target group lists to maintain leads via search and social contacts is ideal for personalization.

✓ AI is also worthwhile for publishing content that needs to be presented in the right networks at the right time.

Conclusion

The age of the revolution of artificial intelligence has already arrived. Clever SEO strategists benefit from this development. The majority of AI systems are not visible, but this does not reduce their value. The search landscape is in a continuous development process. In addition, consumers produce gigantic amounts of data that can be transformed into practical findings. Accordingly, automation can help to understand these insights and give SEO strategists the opportunity to transform them into innovative and personalized strategies.

Do not forget your free SEO-Analysis for further information.
Get it now **www.seomarkt.de/premium**
Password: **SEO2019DE89**

Made in the USA
Middletown, DE
21 December 2019